COMBAT KNIVES

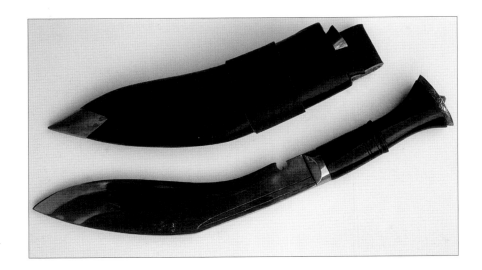

GREENHILL MILITARY MANUALS

COMBAT KNIVES

GREENHILL MILITARY MANUALS

Leroy Thompson

Greenhill Books, London
Stackpole Books, Pennsylvania

Greenhill Books

Combat Knives
First published 2004 by Greenhill Books, Lionel Leventhal Limited, Park House, 1 Russell Gardens, London NW11 9NN
www.greenhillbooks.com
and
Stackpole Books, 5067 Ritter Road, Mechanicsburg, PA 17055, USA

British Library Cataloguing in Publication Data
Thompson, Leroy
Combat knives. – (Greenhill military manuals)
1. Knives
2. Daggers
I. Title
623.4'41

ISBN 1-85367-614-4

Library of Congress Cataloging-in-Publication Data available

Designed by John Anastasio
Printed and bound in Singapore

Cover Photo – Members of the Italian Special Forces unit "Col Moschin" practice knife combat with their Extrema Ratio fighting knives. (Extrema Ratio USA/Frank Miller)

Contents

Introduction

U.S. Ranger in World War II sharpens his fighting knife. (USNA)

Fixed-Blade Combat Knives

Although the earliest primitive stone knives were primarily scraping implements, they no doubt received at least minimal use as weapons. The first really effective fighting knives, however, were probably fabricated of copper. Later came the more effective bronze daggers and short swords which were widely used in ancient warfare. The earliest iron daggers appear to have been constructed of meteor iron, an expensive source but one that gave the weapons a special cachet of having been sent by the gods. Of course, the fact they were constructed of iron made them more durable than bronze as well.

As iron and then steel became more common so did the dagger. By the Middle Ages, excellent steel daggers were available, even to the merchant class, and it was from then on that the knife became the most ubiquitous of weapons. Professional soldiers, knights or men-at-arms carried the dagger as a secondary weapon on the battlefield, one with which a fallen enemy could be dispatched or which gave some ability to keep fighting if their principal weapon was lost or broken.

Off the battlefield, merchants, courtiers, ladies and knights carried the dagger as a self-defense weapon, though the knight normally still carried his sword as well.

Because the dagger was such a ubiquitous weapon during the Middle Ages, myriad types were available. Among the more common were the rondel, baselard and quillon daggers, the latter a type of miniature sword. Other specialist daggers of the early Renaissance included the Italian sword-breaking dagger which incorporated teeth for catching a sword blade, or the bombardier's stiletto which combined a defensive weapon with a measuring device for powder since the blade contained graduated markings.

From the 15th to 18th centuries, the dagger remained the most popular personal weapon, though the increased use of firearms and the availability of relatively small pistols began to infringe upon the dagger's traditional role by the late 18th century. The unreliability of flint and even percussion firearms, however, helped the dagger retain its place as a last line of self-defense. At least some early pocket pistols, in fact, incorporated a built-in folding dagger as an adjunct weapon.

British Commando during World War II carries his F-S dagger on his calf. (IWM)

By the 19th century, the Industrial Revolution had allowed centers of high-quality production knives to develop in Sheffield, Solingen and elsewhere. As a result, high-quality fighting knives were available in certain popular designs. One design that saw substantial usage, particularly in the British Empire, was the Shakespeare knife, designed by an Indian Army officer as a utility- and hunting knife but also serving as an effective double-edged combat knife. Perhaps the most famous knife of the 19th century was the massive Bowie knife, beloved of Americans in the south and west. Another popular type of knife was the naval dirk designed for use by officers and some other ranks during boarding operations in the age of fighting sail. An important innovation of the production knife-makers of Sheffield and Solingen was the folding combat knife, especially the folding dirks or Bowies. The U.S. Army began to purchase specialized combat knives for its troops during the 19th century as industrialization made it possible to expect uniform quality in production knives. The 1849 Ames Rifleman's Knife was the first general issue U.S. military knife and with its double-edged blade was effective as a fighting knife as well as a utility knife. At least partially due to the reliability of cartridge firearms, however, the fighting knife lost popularity by the turn of the century, though a couple of decades later the trench warfare of the First World War would make the fighting knife a prized possession of the infantryman once again.

Prior to the 20th century, traditional daggers had evolved in Africa and Asia as well. Among the more famous of these daggers are the *Kindjal* in the Caucasus,

One of W. E. Fairbairn's favorite close-combat weapons was the smatchet. (IWM)

the *Kukri* in Nepal but known around the world because of its service with Gurkha soldiers, the *Pesh-kabz* in Persia, the *Golok* and *Kris* in Malaya, the *Jambayi* in Arabia, the *Katar* in India, and the *Tanto* and *Hamidashi* in Japan. In some cases, as with the *Jambayi* in Arabia, these traditional daggers are still worn with traditional dress. In other cases, as with the Gurkha *Kukri*, the traditional weapon has evolved into an effective close-combat weapon still widely used today. Other weapons, such as the *Tanto*, have achieved worldwide distribution.

Although some of these eastern weapons saw combat in the early 20th century in the Russo-Japanese War, where Cossacks used the kindjal and Japanese soldiers used traditional swords or daggers, it was still the western front in the First World War that offered the impetus for development of myriad types of close-combat weapons, including fighting knives.

Once the First World War degenerated into static trench warfare, it became apparent that within the confines of a trench system, a rifle with bayonet mounted was hard to wield. Since much trench raiding took place at night, the

At far right an officer wears the distinctive dagger of the First Special Service Force. (USNA)

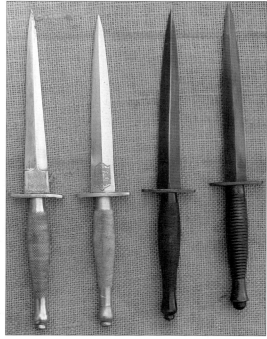

Variations of the Fairbairn-Sykes dagger.

use of handguns was also often difficult, as there was frequently as much chance of killing friend as foe. Instead, hand-to-hand fighting with brass knuckles or knives became the norm. The Germans were issued or had purchased

specialized trench knives, often resembling short versions of the Mauser bayonet. Allied troops who captured these knives made good use of them and also demanded trench knives of their own.

British troops were not issued trench knives, but there were some highly effective weapons available for private purchase such as the Shakespeare or the distinctive short Cledd, the traditional Welsh sword, fabricated at the request of

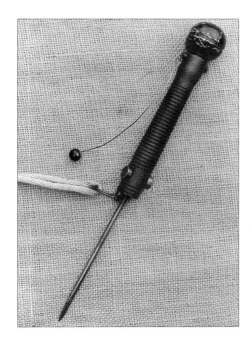

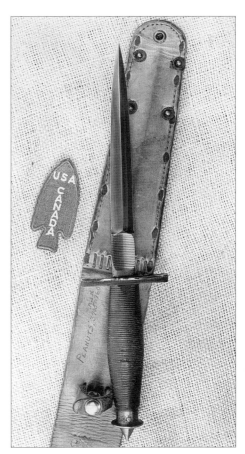

The M-P Close Combat Device combined a dagger, garrote and cosh in one weapon.

Nepali craftsman fabricating a Kukri. (Himalayan Imports)

V-42 stiletto of the First Special Service Force.

Lord Howard de Walden for members of the Welsh Fusiliers under his command. Another interesting First World War design was the Officer's Knife, available from Cogswell and Harrison, and showing similar features to the later Fairbairn-Sykes knife.

American troops were issued two primary types of trench knives: the Model 1917 with a spiked blade, and the M1918 M1 Trench Knife with a double-edged blade. Both incorporated a knuckle duster hand guard. Throughout the "Banana Wars" fought by U.S. Marines between the World Wars, these same trench knives continued to be prized for close combat. Other troops involved in colonial warfare often retained their First World War trench knives as well.

As a result, when the Second World War began, most fighting knives were either left over from the First World War or were newly produced examples of an older design. German infantrymen, for example, continued to carry a *Kampfmesser* very similar to those used in the First World War. German and Italian soldiers and officials also reinstated the old style of carrying dress daggers, though these ornate blades could serve as combat weapons if necessary. In countries occupied by the Germans, members of the Resistance often used locally fabricated combat knives. Among Dutch Commandos fighting for the British and members of the Dutch Underground, the indigenous Model 1915 trench knife retained its popularity during the Second World War.

The array of combat knives available to Allied troops can be attributed to

Contra rebels carry various combat knives to help them survive in the Central American jungle.

The author using a Himalayan Imports kukri for chopping.

Various fighting techniques are practiced with the combat knife. (Cold Steel)

various factors. The development of specialized raiding units such as the Commandos, SAS, Rangers, Marine Raiders, and First Special Service Force created a desire for specialized close-combat blades for use in silent killing but also to help develop the aggressive spirit required of such units. As a result, the Fairbairn-Sykes dagger, the Marine

Raider stiletto, and the V-42 stiletto were all produced. Eventually, the Fairbairn-Sykes knife would be supplied or sold to members of virtually every Allied unit. Other specialized blades were developed for the SOE and OSS to give clandestine warriors compact concealed weapons. Among these were arm daggers, thumb daggers, instep daggers and lapel daggers. In the U.S. armed forces, the First World War tradition of issuing specialized fighting knives continued with the M3 Trench Knife and the Ka-Bar fighting/utility knife, so beloved of the Marines.

Many of the Second World War-era fighting knives remained in service during the early post-war campaigns in Korea, Indochina, Malaya and Kenya. Personnel who remained as professional soldiers often retained the Fairbairn-Sykes dagger or Ka-Bar fighting knife with which they were familiar. New personnel were often issued these proven designs. On counterinsurgency campaigns carried out in jungles, the machete or heavy-duty chopping knife often served as both utility tool and weapon. Upon the partition of India, some Gurkha regiments chose to join the Indian Army, while others joined the British Army; all retained their *kukris*. The Special Air Service was involved in counterinsurgency campaigns in Malaya,

The boot knife has been carried as a hideout weapon for well over a century. (Cold Steel)

Borneo, Aden and Oman, but it was in Borneo that this unit began to use the *Golok* in large numbers. The *Golok* has remained popular with members of the SAS until the present day. Among U.S. troops, the Ka-Bar remained popular, as did the closely related U.S. Navy knife and the similar Jet Pilot's Survival Knife.

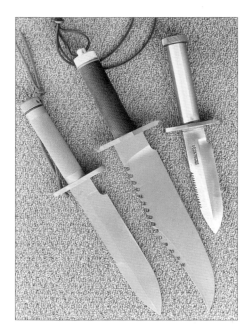

Three examples of the hollow-handled survival knife; left to right: Randall, Lile and Parrish.

Both would remain in service with U.S. or other soldiers and be copied into the 21st century.

During the Cold War, various Warsaw Pact countries developed quite effective combat knives. The Soviets had various knives intended for airborne troops or *Spetsnaz*, including what is often termed the "ballistic knife", which is designed to fire its blade at an enemy using a powerful spring. More widely issued to Soviet troops was a fighting/survival knife with saw-teeth. The Czechs developed some effective paratroop knives and other combat knives as did the East Germans and the Poles.

One of the most interesting, effective and cost-effective combat knives used by NATO countries is the Glock knife, produced for the Austrian armed forces and other military units by the well-known maker of the Glock pistol.

In other parts of the world, combat knives often reflect local traditions. In Colombia, for example, special operations troops carry a combat knife with a hooked blade, which is based on a traditional banana-cutting knife. In Asia, China has issued a wide variety of military or police knives. The knife issued to members of special police units, for example, is worn on the belt in a very short sheath, as much of the blade collapses into the handle in wear. Upon drawing the knife, the blade extends and locks into position.

Another trend, which has produced some very effective knife designs, is that of updating and improving classic combat knives. The Applegate-Fairbairn knife and Smatchet offer

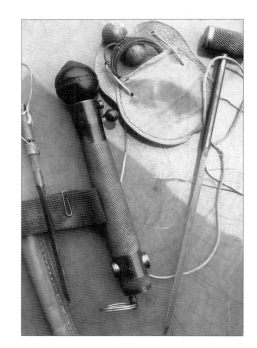

The M-P Close-Combat Device with other clandestine weapons.

excellent examples. Within the U.S. armed forces, the current emphasis on using special operations forces around the world to fight terrorism has caused a great resurgence of interest in high-quality combat knives and specialized blade training. Many

The hollow-handled survival knife allows the carry of useful survival items.

The Skean Dubh is a traditional stocking dagger; shown are three regimental examples.

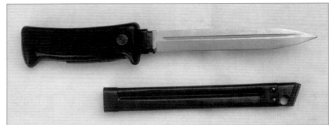

Chinese combination knife and folding pistol stock. (Eric Larsen)

Chinese knife/pistol stock folded for attachment to a Mauser M96 pistol. (Eric Larsen)

Various examples of the Tanto from Cold Steel. (Cold Steel)

military personnel purchase good quality production combat knives such as those from SOG, Gerber, Cold Steel, Kershaw or Katz Knives. Others, however, are willing to spend their own money to purchase a finely crafted custom knife designed to last throughout a military career. Randall-made knives continue to be sought after among military personnel as

they have from the Second World War to Iraq.

The appreciation for custom combat knives has spread to other armed forces as well. Members of the Special Air Service and other British airborne or special forces units have purchased knives from the makers just mentioned, as have personnel in Canada, Australia, France, Belgium, Germany and numerous other countries. The twenty-first century may be the century of

smart weapons and high-tech warfare, but the conflicts in Afghanistan and Iraq have shown once again that the troops at the sharp end may have to rely on a sharp edge to survive! In the mountains of Afghanistan, the deserts of Iraq, and the jungles of the Philippines, U.S., British and Allied troops fighting the war against terrorism have found that the combat knife remains the most effective silent killing weapon for infiltration missions.

Folding Combat and Utility Knives and Automatic Knives

Folding knives are generally dated to the Roman Empire when they were widely employed for eating, general usage and combat. Over the centuries, folding knives remained popular as convenient general-purpose knives, though, until locking blades were developed, they were not particularly effective for close combat.

Although there have been assorted blade types used on folding knives over the centuries, by the beginning of the 20th century, the most widely used were the following:

1. **Spear Point:** in which the spine and cutting edge come to meet each other symmetrically; this type of point is fairly strong and versatile.
2. **Drop Point:** in which there is a more pronounced curve on the cutting edge and less pronounced on the spine; this type is generally used for hunting and skinning
3. **Clip Point:** in which the edge comes up to meet a concave curve from the spine to form a sharp point; this is a versatile blade, able to cut or pierce.
4. **Sheep's Foot Point:** in which a straight cutting edge is combined

A group of folding or automatic knives applicable to police or military usage.

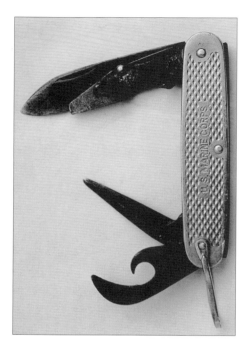

A USMC issue folding knife.

with a spine that curves down to meet it; good for cutting leather, canvas, rubber, rope, etc. Traditionally sailors' knives have used this type of point.

5. **Spey Point:** in which the point is almost a blunter drop point; originally designed for castrating livestock but good for cutting fleshy material in general.

6. **Chisel/Tanto Point:** in which the edge meets the spine by angling up towards it to form a very sharp, strong piercing point; this design is very good for close combat.

By the First World War, folding knives were issued in many armies and navies, often in a variety designed to meet the needs of specialized troops. Sailors' knives in the US and British navies usually had either a square point or sheep's foot point and incorporated a marlinspike. There was, for example, a specialized U.S. Medical Officer's folding knife that incorporated a saw blade. In the years after the First World War, a special folding knife was designed for members of the U.S. Army Signal Corps that incorporated a screwdriver blade and a wire stripper.

By the Second World War, most armies and navies were issuing some type of folding knife to their personnel. In addition to general-purpose pocket knives and those designed for military specialties such as those already mentioned for medical or signals personnel, the development of clandestine special operations forces generated another type of folding knife – the escape knife. Designed to aid OSS or SOE operatives to escape from an enemy if captured, these specialized folding knives incorporated wire cutters and hacksaw blades.

Over the last quarter century, the folding knife has assumed greater importance as a close-combat weapon as martial artists, military personnel, and undercover law enforcement officers have realized its potential. Military and police users have often chosen larger folding fighting knives, such as Spyderco's Military or Police models which have blades of 4.25 inches. Undercover police officers or civilians who carry a folding knife for self defense, however, may choose a smaller knife which can be hidden in the hand, then deployed if needed. Martial artists and undercover police officers have shown special interest in some hooked "Hawk's Bill" folding fighting knives such as Spyderco's Civilian and Matriarch models. Unlike many folding combat knives, which can function as general-purpose knives or close-combat weapons, the Hawk's Bill style is strictly a fighting knife.

Other folding knives which have developed a following among military or police personnel or civilians who carry a folding combat knife are Emerson's Tanto Point CQC7 (a special favorite of mine), Benchmade's

The folding or automatic knife can be especially useful for police tactical officers.

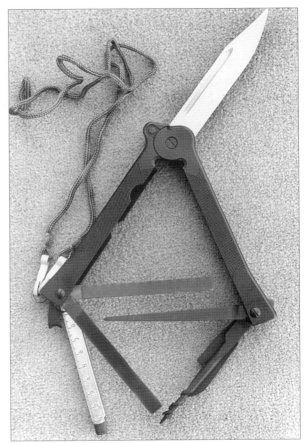

Polish automatic knife issued to paratroopers; this knife also functions as a multi-purpose utility knife.

Pardue Axis Tanto, Cold Steel's Vaquaro and Recon Tanto, Gerber's Applegate-Fairbairn and Spectre, Colombia River's M-16 series, Al Mar's SERE II, SOG's assisted opening Flash 2, Kershaw's Ken Onion, Katz's Kaga Musha, Timberline's Large Worden, Extrema Ratio's Fulcrum, and Masters of Defense's CQD.

Another common use for the folding knife is as a pocket survival tool. For those who work in the outdoors, on a boat or fly in the wilderness, serve in the military, perform law enforcement in rural areas, or others who might find themselves caught in the outdoors, the compact survival kit can prove very useful. At least a few folding knives have been sold which actually incorporate survival items under the scales, but in most cases, the folding knife is a key component of a pocket or pouch survival kit, which includes fire-starting items and other necessities. Probably the most common survival knife is the Swiss Army Knife, which can perform multiple functions.

Another important development was the one-handed opening feature pioneered by Spyderco. The most popular and best known type of one-hand-opening knife is the automatic

knife or switchblade. Designed to be opened by pressing a button or lever that releases the blade, which has been held under spring tension, this type of knife is actually much older than generally assumed.

Certainly the 21st century offers the greatest choice in the history of folding knives. Whether one wants a utility knife to perform everyday tasks, a fighting knife which is easily concealed, a survival knife for use by explorers, outdoorsmen or military personnel, or a special purpose knife such as those used by rescue personnel, the choice today is extensive. Not only that but the buyer can choose among a wide array of high quality production folding knives as well as custom examples. For traditionalists, well-crafted examples of traditional blades that have been in use for centuries are available, while for those who prefer knives that incorporate the latest innovations, high-tech examples abound.

A group of folding knives which may be used for various combat missions.

Multi-Purpose Tools

Perhaps the most useful of edged implements are those tools designed to perform various functions which help their wielder alter his or her environment for comfort or survival. As I write this chapter, in fact, television newscasts are filled with coverage of a hiker who was forced to amputate his own arm with a pocket multi-tool in order to save his life. Although this is certainly an extreme use of a multi-purpose tool, it is indicative of the creative uses to which such devices may be put.

Although the Swiss Army Knife has remained primarily a pocketknife, but which incorporates some tools, the Multi-Tool is generally based on a pair of pliers that incorporate other blades and tools. The Second World War OSS/SOE Escape Knife incorporates pliers as well as hacksaws, but the contemporary multi-tool owes its genesis to the Leatherman Tool developed towards the end of the 1970s.

Among military multi-purpose survival/utility tools, those for aircrew are usually the most versatile. The one issued to Russian aircrew combines an ax, hammer, screwdriver, saw and shovel and is quite well designed.

A very useful general-purpose survival tool is what is sometimes

Although the Swiss Army Knife can perform many functions, the various multi-tools have the advantage of incorporating pliers as well as other tools.

termed the "*Spetsnaz Machete*". Issued to Soviet special operations troops, this tool was designed so it could be used to chop, saw, pry, dig and cut. It also incorporates a hollow handle to allow survival items to be carried. Additional attachments include an ice pick, which may be affixed to the butt. As with many other edged implements, Russian *Spetsnaz* and airborne troops have trained to use this tool as a weapon as well.

Another utility item also used as a weapon by Russian troops is the entrenching tool. Although primarily intended for digging, when sharpened the entrenching tool has often proven a wicked close-combat weapon. Both Russian and U.S. troops have traditionally sharpened their entrenching tools for use in close combat. The U.S. tool issued in Vietnam was used more than once when the Viet Cong penetrated firebases or other installations and hand-to-hand combat was required. Russian airborne and *Spetsnaz* not only practice close combat movements with the entrenching tool but also learn to throw it, much as a throwing ax might be used. In fact, Cold Steel offers a Special Forces Shovel which is based on the Russian airborne/*Spetsnaz* model and which works quite well as a weapon or tool.

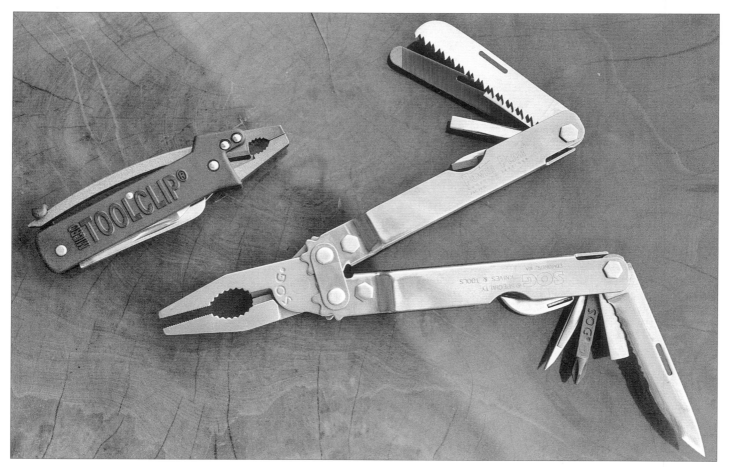

Multi-tools come in various sizes to fit the needs of each user.

Entrenching tools have also seen other uses. In Second World War jungle fighting, for example, U.S. Marines or Army infantrymen sometimes had one man keep his shovel at hand at night for scooping up grenades and hurling them from within their foxholes or shoving them into a recess dug for disposal of grenades. How successful this tactic normally was is debatable, but it may well have worked on occasion and it likely raised morale. Additionally, the shovel could be used against a Japanese soldier at close range.

Other tools designed for use in building trenches have also served as weapons as well. In the First World War, the French issued a curved hacking tool designed for cutting fascines, but it proved an effective close-combat weapon. The combination pickax/shovel issued to U.S. troops not only allowed foxholes to be dug in hard ground more readily but also proved a useful weapon.

Even in this age of high-tech warfare, the entrenching tool remains an extremely important piece of equipment to the infantryman. Whether facing artillery, air power, mortars, rockets, or small-arms fire, the entrenching tool grants the infantryman the ability to create cover where none exists.

Another multi-purpose tool encountered with police or military special units is the Hallagan or "Hooligan" tool. Designed for use during building entries and clearing to gain rapid entry, the Hallagan may be used for prying, battering or penetrating and is normally non-sparking and non-conductive for use around electrical wires and in hazardous environments. Firms such as Dynamic Entry offer not only the Hallagan tool but various other specialized entry tools. Another useful yet simple entry tool is an incredibly tough pry bar from Mad Dog Knives, which was developed for various special operations applications. Mad Dog also makes a Mirage-X pry bar of ceramic composite that is corrosion-proof, non-conductive, and non-magnetic. As a result, this pry bar is particularly useful for those with an Explosives Ordnance Disposal Mission and also for those who raid clandestine drug labs where the danger of fire or contact with chemicals is high.

Ranking with the entrenching tool in ubiquity among military personnel is the machete or one of its relatives. Although primarily intended for clearing the way through heavy brush or jungle, the machete has also proven to be an exceptional close-combat weapon. Many cultures that developed in a jungle environment have some traditional hacking implement akin to the machete,

including such blades as the *Panang*, *Bolo*, or *Golok*. Dozens of variations of the machete have been issued to military units around the world, some reflecting the conditions in which they were intended for use, while others have reflected traditional designs. In some cases, other agricultural implements with a similar function have assumed a military mission. In some Latin American countries, for example, the traditional heavy banana-cutting knife is used as a military utility tool.

During the Second World War, especially in the Asian theater, the machete proved a quite effective close-combat weapon in addition to performing its primary function of clearing a path through the jungle. Among the machetes issued within the U.S. armed forces were the Collins Army machete, the USMC machete that had a cleaver style blade which proved effective at close combat as well, the Signal Corps Machete, and the OSS Machete.

Some traditional implements seem to reinvent themselves in warfare again and again. The tomahawk, for example, was carried by America's first "élite" unit, Rogers Rangers, during the French and Indian Wars, yet is still used by some special operations forces in Afghanistan 250 years later.

Becker Knife and Tool Combat Bowie "Desert Series"

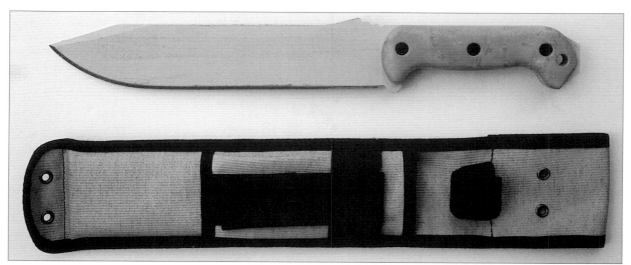

Becker Knife and Tool Combat Bowie

This heavy-duty combat knife is designed for those military personnel who want a big, tough knife for utility chores yet which can be fearsome in close combat. Its .210-thick 0170-6 high-carbon-steel blade is designed to stand up to hard usage and hold its edge. Despite the Combat Bowie's size, it is very well balanced for hacking or slashing. The serration atop the spine makes an especially good thumb rest for more precise usage. The combination of the desert tan blade, grip and sheath tailor it very well for U.S. troops fighting in the desert environment, and it has proven itself quite popular with combat soldiers.

Overall Length: 14.5 inches
Blade Length: 9 inches
Weight: 18.3 ounces
Blade Type: Drop Point Bowie with desert tan thermally-cured polymer coating
Grip: GV6H polymer, desert camo, with wrist-thong hole
Crossguard: Lower, integral
Sheath: Desert tan, nylon with utility pocket, tie-down holes
Source: Camillus Cutlery Company, 54 Main Street, Camillus, NY 13031, (315) 672-8111, www.camillusknives.com

Benchmade Nimravus

Benchmade Nimravus

Although Benchmade is best known for producing quality folding knives, the Nimravus is a well-designed, well-made compact fixed-blade combat knife. It is well balanced and incorporates thumb grooves atop the base of the blade for control. The slimness of the knife allows it to be carried very easily, while the sheath is especially well designed for various attachment methods. The combination of the well-fitted Kydex sheath and the release lever, which is easily pushed off by the thumb as the knife is drawn, offer excellent retention when worn in the upside-down position on webbed gear.

Overall Length: 9.5 inches
Blade Length: 4.5 inches
Weight: 6.2 ounces

Blade Type: Clip Point, partially serrated
Grip: G10 panels, finger-grooved, exposed tang with hole for wrist thong
Crossguard: Small integral
Sheath: Molded Kydex with additional retention lever
Source: Benchmade Knife Company, 300 Beaver Creek Rd., Oregon City, OR 97045, (503) 656-6004, www.benchmade.com

Blackjack Grunt

Knifeware knives are designed and marketed by well-known knife writer and editor Ken Warner and reflect his years of experience with blades. They are designed to offer tough, usable knives at a reasonable price. The Grunt incorporates a blade well designed for outdoorsmen but also applicable as a combat/utility knife. Balance is good and the AUS-8 steel blade holds an edge well. The Warrior, which is discussed later, is a better pure combat knife, but the Grunt is more versatile and compact.

Overall Length: 11 inches
Blade Length: 5.7 inches
Weight: 10 ounces
Blade Type: Slight Drop Point with long curved cutting edge
Crossguard: Lower, integral with grip
Grip: Kraton with wrist-thong hole
Sheath: Leather with retention strap, belt loop, and three lacing holes for alternative carry
Source: Knifeware, Inc., P.O. Box 3, Greenville, WV 24945, (304) 832-6878, www.knifeware.com

Blackjack Grunt

Boker Applegate-Fairbairn Fighting Knife

Boker Applegate-Fairbairn Fighting Knife

Applegate sent me an early prototype of this knife until the present, I have rated it quite highly as a close-combat knife.

Overall Length: 10.8 inches
Blade Length: 6 inches
Weight: 8.6 ounces
Blade Type: Double-edged Spear Point, facsimiles of signatures of W. E. Fairbairn and Rex Applegate
Grip: Molded Lexon with ribs and hole for wrist thong
Crossguard: Brass, double-sided and angled downward
Sheath: Kydex with rubber retention loop (leather also available with Velcro loop)
Source: Boker, Solingen; Boker USA, Inc., 1550 Balsam St., Lakewood, CO 80214-5917, (303) 462-0662, www.bokerusa.com

The Applegate-Fairbairn is the improved and evolved version of the classic F-S Commando Dagger based upon wartime conversations between Rex Applegate and W. E. Fairbairn. Its design was intended to correct the problems that arose with the F-S during Second World War combat. First, the original F-S dagger's point had a tendency to break off about .25-inch to .5-inch from the tip. As a result, the point of the A-F is much sturdier. The original F-S also had a tendency to turn in the hand and to not allow quick orientation of the cutting edge in the dark. The flattened grip of the A-F helps eliminate this problem. Using matte 440C stainless steel for the A-F's blade also enhances durability. The original production of the A-F incorporated lead weights in the handle to allow the user to adjust balance to his or her individual tastes, but later production examples dispensed with this feature. It remains a well balanced knife. From the time when Rex

Boker Applegate-Fairbairn Smatchet

As with the S-F Fighting Knife, the A-F Smatchet is an improved variant of the Second World War version. W. E. Fairbairn believed that the Smatchet was one of the most deadly edged weapons ever created and trained the Commandos and other personnel to use it to devastating effect. The issue Second World War model, however, used relatively thin steel for the blade and crossguard which did not stand up to the heavy use to which the weapons were sometimes subjected. The S-F Smatchet is a heavy-duty weapon and implement, yet is quite well balanced and lively in the hand when used for close combat.

Overall Length: 15.8 inches
Blade Length: 10 inches
Weight: 19.8 ounces
Blade Type: Double-edged Spear Point
Grip: Polymer, ribbed with wrist-thong hole
Crossguard: Integral with blade and grip
Sheath: Ballistic nylon
Source: Boker, Solingen; Boker USA, Inc., 1550 Balsam St., Lakewood, CO 80214-5917, (303) 462-0662, www.bokerusa.com

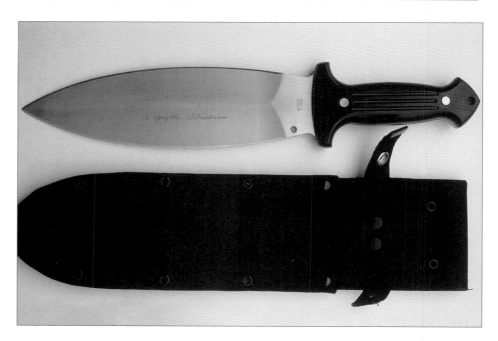

Boker Applegate-Fairbairn Smatchet

Boker Orca

Boker Orca

The Orca is designed as a heavy-duty knife for combat swimmers and has been used by the German counter-terrorist unit GSG-9. It also makes a relatively good general-purpose combat knife as well. The secondary chopping edge on the top portion of the blade is a useful feature, especially since this is a sturdily built knife, which can take hard use.

Overall Length: 10.3 inches
Blade Length: 5 inches
Weight: 11.7 ounces
Blade Type: Drop Point, with partially serrated edge and chopping edge atop blade
Crossguard: Integral with grip
Grip: Molded polymer with ridges and double holes for wrist loop or line
Sheath: Polymer with rubber retaining ring, retention lever lock, and rubber arm/leg straps
Source: Boker, Solingen; Boker USA, Inc.,1550 Balsam St., Lakewood, CO 80214-5917, (303) 462-0662, www.bokerusa.com

Buck Nighthawk

One of the first things one notices with the Nighthawk is its very ergonomic grip, especially the built-in thumb rest atop the hilt. It is a good fighting knife that can also serve as a general-purpose combat knife. Unfortunately, the sheath is not as well designed for combat as the knife, as it lacks secondary retention for wearing inverted and is not designed to affix easily to webbed gear.

Overall Length: 11.3 inches
Blade Length: 6.5 inches
Weight: 10 ounces
Blade Type: Clip Point
Crossguard: Lower, upper thumb rest
Grip: Black/olive reinforced molded nylon, rubberized, non-slip pebbling
Sheath: Ballistic nylon with retention strap
Source: Buck Knives Inc., 1900 Weld Blvd., El Cajon, CA 92020, (619) 449-1100, www.buckknives.com

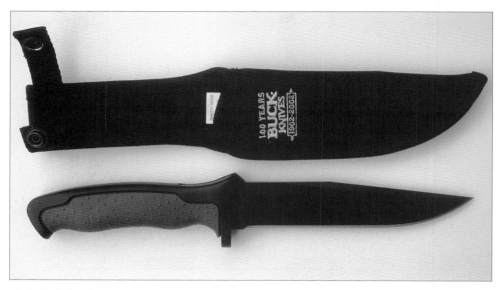

Buck Nighthawk

Buck Strider Tactical

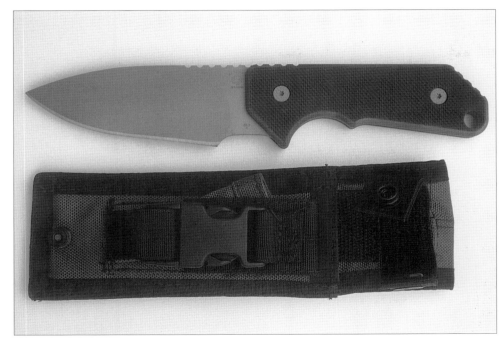

Buck Strider Tactical

designed for combat usage also, though the single retention strap does not offer additional security if the knife is carried upside-down on webbed gear or equipment. The belt loop attachment using Velcro does allow it to be affixed or removed quickly from the belt.

Overall Length: 9.8 inches
Blade Length: 4.8 inches
Weight: 11.2 ounces
Blade Type: Drop Point, single-edged
Crossguard: None
Grip: G10, checkered, front finger groove, wrist-thong hole
Sheath: Cordura with Kydex liner, pocket for sharpening stone, retention strap
Source: Buck Knives Inc., 1900 Weld Blvd., El Cajon, CA 92020, (619) 449-1100, www.buckknives.com

This is a very sturdy combat knife with a blade designed to stand up to hard usage. Ridges atop the blade and grip and at the rear of the grip are designed to allow additional force to be applied with the palm or fist. The sheath is well

Camillus Jet Pilots' Survival Knife

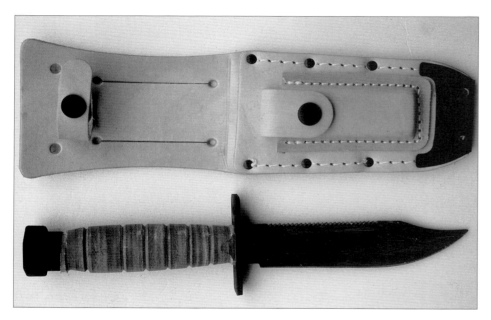

Camillus Jet Pilots' Survival Knife

service, yet still capable of use in close combat. The sheath design allows the Jet Pilots' Knife to be carried upside-down on webbed gear, affixed to a survival vest, or on a belt. As a basic aircrew survival knife, this is a proven design that offers excellent value.

Overall Length: 9.7 inches
Blade Length: 5.2 inches
Weight: 8.6 ounces
Blade Type: Clip Point, serrated on spine
Crossguard: Double, squared, with tie-down holes
Grip: Stacked leather washers with steel butt for hammering
Sheath: Leather with pocket for sharpening stone, snap retention strap, and lacing holes
Source: Camillus Cutlery Company, 54 Main Street, Camillus, NY 13031, (315) 672-8111, www.camillusknives.com

The Jet Pilots' Knife has been issued to U.S. military aviators in some form since 1957 when Navy Pilots first adopted it, though this original version had a blade that was one inch longer. Although other makers have produced this knife on military contracts, Camillus has produced it for decades and still offers the traditional knife for sale. I have always had a special affection for this knife since I used one for a time in Vietnam. As with many widely issued military knives, this one is fairly basic, but it is a nice size to fit on a pilot's survival vest while still offering a knife tough enough for utility

Camillus USMC Knife

Camillus USMC Knife

For generations of U.S. Marines, orders to sharpen this knife have been a good indicator that they were going into combat. Known generically as the "Ka-Bar" after one of its manufacturers, this fighting knife has been used by Marines now for sixty years and has seen combat wherever the Marines have landed. Camillus still makes this traditional knife, though the Second World War Ka-Bars had the crossguards slightly bent towards the pommel, while this Camillus uses a straight crossguard. The Marines traditionally love their "Ka-Bars", the only criticisms usually arising from misusing the knife in utility tasks, which can cause the point to break. One advantage of this utility knife, however, is that it is relatively inexpensive to replace yet still gives good service. The number of ex-Marines who are still using their "Ka-Bars" decades after leaving the Corps attests to its durability.

Overall Length: 12 inches
Blade Length: 7 inches
Weight: 10.2 ounces
Blade Type: Bowie, Clip Point
Crossguard: Double
Grip: Stacked leather washers
Sheath: Leather, snap retention strap, tie-down hole
Source: Camillus Cutlery Company, 54 Main Street, Camillus, NY 13031, (315) 672-8111, www.camillusknives.com

Chinese Armed Police Knife

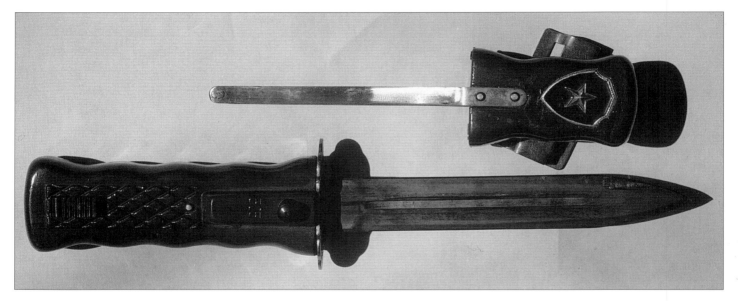

Chinese Armed Police Knife

Although some elements of the Peoples' Republic of China's police are armed with firearms, many patrol officers are not. At least some of these are armed with this interesting fighting knife. Designed so that it is not obviously a knife when worn on the belt, since the grip and sheath fit together and the blade collapses into the grip, in wear this is a very compact knife. Not designed for heavy military combat usage, this knife is instead intended for self-defense should the police officer be attacked while performing his or her duties. Apparently, officers are trained in some basic martial arts movements using this blade.

Overall Length: 9.6 inches
Blade Length: 5.3 inches
Weight: 5.8 ounces
Blade Type: Telescoping Spear Point
Crossguard: Integral with grip
Grip: Polymer
Sheath: Polymer with belt clip
Source: Chinese State Factories.

Cold Steel OSS

Cold Steel OSS

The combination of the sub-hilt, which keeps the hand in position during thrusts, and the double edge allows the OSS to be used very effectively in close combat. Because the blade is relatively light for its length, it is very fast, but in combination with the rather fine point does not make it a good utility knife. The OSS is a killing knife. The sheath offers various options for carrying the knife including standard belt loop, loops built into the sheath for other strap attachment, and holes for lacing onto gear.

Overall Length: 13.5 inches
Blade Length: 8.3 inches
Weight: 8.2 ounces
Blade Type: Drop Point, bead-blasted, upper edge sharpened
Crossguard: Integral with grip
Grip: Kraton with sub-hilt, checkered, hole for wrist thong
Sheath: Secure-Ex polymer with snap retention strap and various holes and slots for mounting
Source: Cold Steel, Inc., 3036-A Seaborg Ave., Ventura, CA 93003, (805) 650-8481, www.coldsteel.com

Cold Steel Para Edge

Cold Steel Para Edge

fulfills the same function that compact arm and wrist daggers did for OSS or SOE agents during the Second World War. Though certainly not designed to replace a full-sized fighting knife, it does give a trained wielder an emergency self-defense weapon.

Overall Length: 5.8 inches
Blade Length: 3 inches
Weight: 1.4 ounces
Blade Type: Tanto, partially serrated
Crossguard: Integral with grip
Grip: Kraton with wrist-thong hole
Sheath: Concealex with neck cord and six holes for lacing to equipment
Source: Cold Steel, Inc., 3036-A Seaborg Ave., Ventura, CA 93003, (805) 650-8481, www.coldsteel.com

The Para-Edge Series (double-edged spear point and clip point models are also available) is designed as a light, concealable combat knife which can be worn around the neck or lashed elsewhere about the person. This knife

Cold Steel Recon Tanto

Cold Steel Recon Tanto

The Recon Tanto is very popular with special military and police units who like the toughness and penetration capability of the design. The blackened blade is another desirable feature for special operations usage. The Recon Tanto is heavy enough to be used for hacking as well as thrusting or slashing and, of course, retains the Tanto's ability to penetrate deeply. Cold Steel offers a wide assortment of Tanto designs to fit all sorts of tactical situations. Not all are covered in this work so it might be advisable to check the website to determine which one fits a specific need.

Overall Length: 11.8 inches
Blade Length: 7 inches
Weight: 9 ounces
Blade Type: Tanto, black epoxy powder-coated
Crossguard: Single lower integral with grip
Grip: Kraton, checkered, with wrist-thong hole
Sheath: Leather with double retaining straps and tie-down cord (Concealex also available)
Source: Cold Steel, Inc., 3036-A Seaborg Ave., Ventura, CA 93003, (805) 650-8481, www.coldsteel.com

Cold Steel Spike Tanto

Cold Steel Spike Tanto

The Spike was designed by Barry Dawson and is intended to offer a strong thrusting and slashing weapon in a very narrow blade. This blade is designed as an effective concealment weapon which may be carried in many different ways. At least some military or police personnel carry the Spike as a last ditch close-combat weapon which will penetrate through heavy clothing or gear to deliver a disabling thrust.

Overall Length: 8 inches
Blade Length: 4 inches
Weight: 2.6 ounces

Blade Type: Tanto
Crossguard: None
Grip: Cord wrapping
Sheath: Secure-Ex with neck chain, belt notch, and lashing holes
Source: Cold Steel, Inc., 3036-A Seaborg Ave., Ventura, CA 93003, (805) 650-8481, www.coldsteel.com

Cold Steel Safekeeper II

Cold Steel's push daggers have remained one of their most popular designs because they offer a lot of knife in a compact package. Originally designed as a concealment dagger for gamblers and others in the American west, the push dagger retains its popularity at least partially because it can be used effectively without extensive training. Since it is held with the blade protruding between the fingers, one can deliver thrusts and slashes using a more natural clenched-fist grip. The push dagger may also be thrust with substantial power because of its design. The design can also help deflect cuts delivered at the knife hand, but it does expose the back of the hand to slashes.

Overall Length: 6.4 inches
Blade Length: 3.8 inches
Weight: 3.6 ounces
Blade Type: Double-edged Spear Point, bead-blasted finish
Crossguard: None
Grip: T-grip Kraton
Sheath: Secure-Ex with clip or lacing holes
Source: Cold Steel, Inc., 3036-A Seaborg Ave., Ventura, CA 93003, (805) 650-8481, www.coldsteel.com

Cold Steel Safekeeper II

Cold Steel Tai Pan

Cold Steel Tai Pan

The Tai-Pan is Cold Steel's offering for those who like the double-edged stiletto-style fighting knife. As with the Applegate-Fairbairn, this is an improved version of the traditional Fairbairn-Sykes knife. Unlike thinner bladed stilettos, however, the Tai-Pan has a heavy-duty AUS 8A stainless steel blade. The Tai-Pan is one of my favorites among Cold Steel's extensive line. Although many of those who teach close combat with the blade currently do not stress the use of a skull crusher, since my initial training did include these techniques, I like the fact that the Tai-Pan's pommel functions quite well as an impact and puncturing weapon.

Overall Length: 13 inches
Blade Length: 7.5 inches

Weight: 10.8 ounces
Blade Type: Double-edged Spear Point
Crossguard: Steel, double
Grip: Kraton, checkered, pointed pommel with wrist-thong hole
Sheath: Leather with retaining strap and belt loop
Source: Cold Steel, Inc., 3036-A Seaborg Ave., Ventura, CA 93003, (805) 650-8481, www.coldsteel.com

Extrema Ratio "Col. Moschin"

Supplied to the special operations regiment of the Italian Folgore Brigade, this is an excellent close-combat knife, well balanced and designed for slashes, cuts or thrusts from various positions. The finish, "Testudo", is a black nitrate coating that is very resistant to corrosion, a boon in a special ops knife. The sheath is very well designed to allow mounting in various positions on webbed gear or as a drop sheath on the thigh. The sheath offers good friction retention as well as incorporating a retention strap with a double snap. Italian special ops forces have a long tradition of skill with the blade, so the fact that they have adopted this knife says quite a bit about its quality and design.

Overall Length: 11.4 inches
Blade Length: 6.3 inches
Weight: 9.2 ounces
Blade Type: Stainless cobalt steel, Clip/Tanto, double-edged, partially serrated
Crossguard: Double, integral with blade
Grip: Kraton, Finger Recessed, Extended Tang with Wrist-thong hole

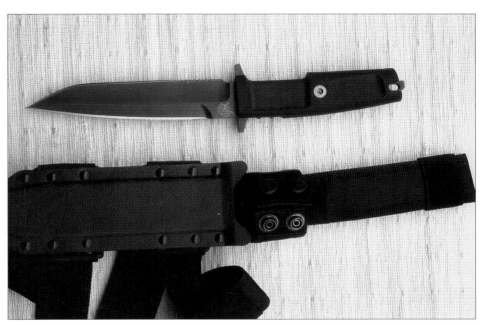

Extrema Ratio "Col. Moschin"

Sheath: Polymer with Six D-Ring Attachments, Leg Straps
Source: Extrema Ratio V.le Montegrappa, 298-59100 Prato (PO), Italy. Telephone: +39 57 458 4639, www.extremaratio.com

US Source: Extrema Ratio USA, 1320 S. Glenstone #26, Springfield, MO 65804, (417) 883-9444, www.extremaratiousa.com

Extrema Ratio Fulcrum

The Fulcrum may be Extrema's most popular combat knife. It is a bit slimmer and lighter than the Golem and is very fast in the hand. This example has the "Testudo" finish, which is designed to be rugged enough for combat swimmers whose weapons face constant immersion in salt water. As with the Golem, the Fulcrum is well designed as a fighting knife but is also tough enough to serve as a military combat/utility knife. As a result, this has proven a popular private purchase military knife, especially among special operations troops.

Overall Length: 12 inches
Blade Length: 7 inches
Weight: 11.4 ounces
Blade Type: Modified Tanto with partial serration
Crossguard: Double, integral with blade
Grip: Kraton, finger recess with extended tang with wrist-thong hole
Sheath: Polymer with six D-ring attachments, leg straps
Source: Extrema Ratio V.le Montegrappa, 298-59100 Prato (PO), Italy. Telephone: +39 57 458 4639, www.extremaratio.com

US Source: Extrema Ratio USA, 1320 S. Glenstone #26, Springfield, MO 65804, (417) 883-9444, www.extremaratiousa.com

Extrema Ratio Fulcrum

Extrema Ratio Golem F

The Golem F has many of the same features as other Extrema Ratio knives including the ergonomic grip. The "F" designation indicates the large teeth along the top edge of the blade, which are available on the Golem and the Harpoon. For those Extrema Ratio knives ordered from the U.S. distributor, kits that allow the blade and sheath to be tailored for desert, arctic or jungle/forest environments are available. These include solid color replacement handles and suitable camouflage sheaths. For the military user who may be deployed to various theaters, a selection of these kits allows for S-V agreement with selection tailoring of his or her fighting knife to the environment in which it will be used.

Overall Length: 12 inches
Blade Length: 7 inches
Weight: 12 ounces
Blade Type: Modified Tanto, with large teeth on upper edge and partial serration on lower, tiger tech camouflage
Crossguard: Double, integral with blade
Grip: Kraton, finger recessed with extended tang and wrist-thong hole

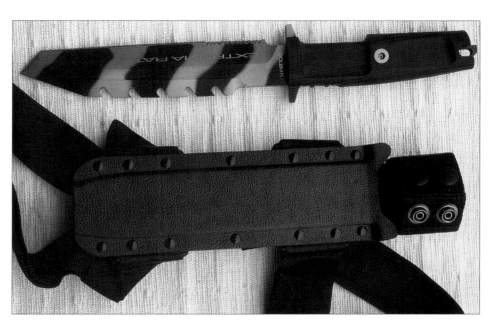

Extrema Ratio Golem F

Sheath: Polymer with six D-ring attachments, leg straps
Source: Extrema Ratio V.le Montegrappa, 298-59100 Prato (PO), Italy. Telephone: +39 57 458 4639, www.extremaratio.com

US Source: Extrema Ratio USA, 1320 S. Glenstone #26, Springfield, MO 65804, (417) 883-9444, www.extremaratiousa.com

Gerber Guardian Back up

The Guardian is the latest in Gerber's line of boot knives. Its double edge and sharp point allow it to be deployed for slashes in either direction, or thrusts. The versatile mounting system incorporated into the sheath allows it to be carried as a true boot-knife clipped inside the boot or lashed or strapped to gear anywhere on the person.

Overall Length: 7 inches
Blade Length: 3.3 inches
Weight: 1.8 ounces
Blade Type: Double-edged Spear Point
Crossguard: Small, double, integral with grip
Grip: Rubber/nylon with slight ribs
Sheath: Polymer with built-in lock, carry clip and double loops for attachment to belt or gear
Source: Gerber Legendary Blades, P.O. Box 23088, Portland, OR 97224 USA, (503) 639-6161, www.gerberblades.com

Gerber Guardian Back Up

Gerber Silver Trident

Gerber Silver Trident

The Silver Trident takes its name from the qualification badge for U.S. Navy SEALs and indicates its intended use by special operations forces, especially combat swimmers. Designed by retired SEAL Master Chief James Watson and knifemaker Bill Harsey, the Silver Trident also incorporates suggestions from SEALs and other special operators. Its overall length and blade length, for example, are designed to be long enough for close combat but short enough for ease of carry and handling, especially underwater. It also incorporates features such as the stainless steel butt cap for hammering and the full width flat atop the blade to allow applying pressure with the hand or fist. The Silver Trident is a very practical special operations knife.

Overall Length: 11.1 inches
Blade Length: 6.2 inches
Weight: 11 ounces
Blade Type: Blackened Clip Point, partially serrated
Crossguard: Large, double
Grip: Contoured Hytrel designed to be comfortable in different-sized hands, non-slip, stainless steel butt cap for hammering, wrist-thong hole
Sheath: Ballistic nylon with utility pocket, tie-down thong, retention lock, and retention strap
Source: Gerber Legendary Blades, P.O. Box 23088, Portland, OR 97224 USA, (503) 639-6161, www.gerberblades.com

Harrison M3

Harrison M3

Fabricated of D-2 steel for all-round toughness, the Harrison M3 is designed to stand up to stresses faced by a general-purpose combat knife. Balance is excellent on this knife, and the grip is well shaped for different holds. As with most custom makers, Harrison can tailor this or his other knives to special needs. Although the sheath is of sturdy construction, for military use I would recommend having a ballistic nylon or Kydex sheath fabricated which would allow the knife to be carried more readily on webbed gear.

Overall Length: 12.3 inches
Blade Length: 7.8 inches
Weight: 11.8 ounces
Blade Type: Spear Point, based on US M3 Fighting Knife
Crossguard: Double, nickel silver
Grip: Black linen Micarta with nickel silver butt cap
Sheath: Leather with thong retention
Source: Dan Harrison Custom Knives, 492 VZCR 4812, Ben Wheeler, TX 75754, (903) 852-3791, e-mail: dwhclh@msn.com

Dan Harrison has been making knives for over fifty years and brings his experience as a combat infantryman and peace officer to his designs. His M3 is meant to be a high quality, sturdier version of the traditional U.S. M3 combat knife.

Himalayan Imports Ang Khola Kukri

Himalayan Imports offers extremely high quality kukris from Nepal, which are hand forged there by Kamis (master bladesmiths). For anyone who has only seen the cheap thin-bladed Kukris normally encountered, these blades are a revelation. Very heavy and sturdy, these Kukris are designed to stand up to a lifetime of hard usage. The Ang Khola makes an excellent utility blade for hacking but it is also a deadly close-combat weapon. Note that the Kukri's dogleg design allows it to deliver a chop with incredible force. Although the Ang Khola shown is the most popular size, 12-inch overall and 20-inch overall versions are also available. The Ang Khola and other Himalayan Imports Kukris are especially popular with U.S. Special Forces and have seen extensive use in Afghanistan and Iraq. The Ang Khola has consistently been the most popular Himalayan Imports blade.

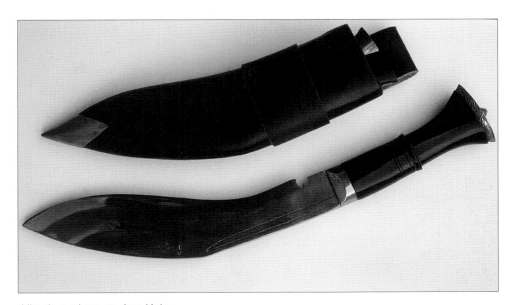

Himalayan Imports Ang Kola

Overall Length: 15 inches
Blade Length: 10 inches
Weight: 25.4 ounces
Blade Type: Traditional Kukri, zone tempered
Crossguard: None
Grip: Water buffalo horn with brass fittings

Sheath: Water buffalo hide with small utility knife and burnishing tool, brass chape
Source: Himalayan Imports, 3495 Lakeside Drive PMB69, Reno, NV 89509, (775) 825-2279, www.himalayan-imports.com

Himalayan Imports British Army Service Kukri

Himalayan Imports British Army Service Kukri

quality. Its blade is a compromise between the heavy-duty Ang Khola and the longer, slimmer fighting Sirupati, which will be discussed next. For close combat, the Army Service Kukri handles a bit more quickly than the Ang Khola but is not quite as heavy for general combat utility usage. Both are excellent knives. This is the second most popular Himalayan Imports Kukri.

Overall Length: 15.5 inches
Blade Length: 10.8 inches
Weight: 22 ounces
Blade Type: Traditional Kukri, zone tempered
Crossguard: None
Grip: Water buffalo horn with brass fittings
Sheath: Water buffalo hide with small utility knife and burnishing tool, brass chape
Source: Himalayan Imports, 3495 Lakeside Drive PMB69, Reno, NV 89509, (775) 825-2279, www.himalayan-imports.com

This Kukri is designed to be similar to the issue knives carried by Gurkhas serving in the British or Indian Armies but far exceeds military specifications in toughness and

Himalayan Imports Sirupati

Sirupati means "leaf pointed" in Nepali and describes the slimmer blade on this fighting Kukri. This lighter, slimmer Kukri is very fast handling and is popular with martial artists who practice with the Kukri. It also is popular with some military units, at least one group of USAF Combat Control Team members in Afghanistan having equipped themselves with them. Although the 20-inch overall Sirupati is illustrated, 12- and 15-inch versions are available as well. I emphasize again that Himalayan Imports Kukris have to be seen to appreciate just how high their quality is.

Overall Length: 20 inches
Blade Length: 15 inches
Weight: 23.6 ounces
Blade Type: Elongated Kukri, zone tempered
Crossguard: None
Grip: Wood with brass fittings
Sheath: Water buffalo hide with small utility knife and burnishing tool, brass chape
Source: Himalayan Imports, 3495 Lakeside Drive PMB69, Reno, NV 89509, (775) 825-2279, www.himalayan-imports.com

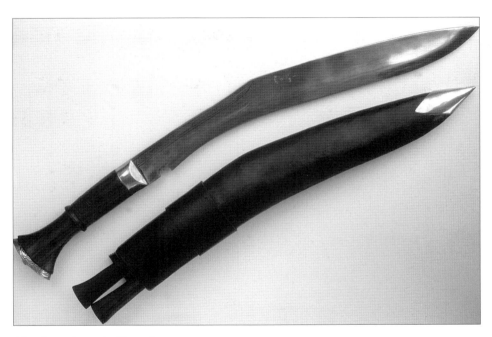

Himalayan Imports Sirupati

Katz Alley Kat

Katz Alley Kat

Although I like all of the Katz Knives I have evaluated, the Alley Kat is my favorite. The grip is very ergonomic and allows various types of grip. The 5-cm blade is thick enough for heavy use in hacking. The double retention straps plus the D-ring on the sheath allow the Alley Kat to be carried in various ways about the webbed gear which lends great versatility. As with other Katz Knives, this one also takes an edge well and holds it.

Overall Length: 13 inches
Blade Length: 8 inches
Weight: 11 ounces
Blade Type: Clip Point with blood groove
Crossguard: Steel, double
Grip: Checkered Kraton with wrist-thong hole
Sheath: Ballistic nylon with two retention straps, D-ring and tie-down thong
Source: Katz Knives, P.O. Box 730, Chandler, AZ 85224, (480) 786-9334, www.katzkn@aol.com

Katz Aristo-Kat

The Aristo-Kat is the largest, heavy-duty version of Katz's Lion King series. This is a big knife suitable for those who need a heavy-duty combat or survival knife capable of standing up to hard usage. The Lion King, which has a 6-inch blade, will probably be more popular for general usage, but there is a trend among some military special ops personnel to carry a utility folding knife and a heavy-duty combat knife such as the Aristo-Kat.

Overall Length: 12.8 inches
Blade Length: 8 inches
Weight: 13.5 ounces
Blade Type: Clip Point with top serration
Crossguard: Single, steel, lower
Grip: Checkered Kraton with steel butt cap and wrist-thong hole
Sheath: Ballistic nylon with D-ring, tie-down thong and single retention strap
Source: Katz Knives, P.O. Box 730, Chandler, AZ 85224, (480) 786-9334, www.katzkn@aol.com

Katz Aristo-Kat

Katz Avenger Boot Knife

Katz Avenger Boot Knife

This is one of the best production boot knives on the market, combining lightness with toughness and good balance. Fabricated of XT-70 stainless steel, the Avenger's blade takes a point well and has high corrosion resistance. It utilizes a grip that is much more comfortable than that of many boot knives and is well designed for use with varying close-combat styles. An alternative sheath for use by divers or other special operations personnel employs two arm/leg straps.

Overall Length: 8.8 inches
Blade Length: 4.5 inches
Weight: 6.5 ounces
Blade Type: Spear Point, with blood groove and serration
Crossguard: Double, steel
Grip: Kraton, wrist-thong hole
Sheath: Ballistic nylon with clip and D-ring, single retaining strap
Source: Katz Knives, P.O. Box 730, Chandler, AZ 85224, (480) 786-9334, www.katzkn@aol.com

Kershaw Amphibian Boot Knife

The Amphibian is cleverly designed to save weight yet offer a tough little combat knife. Constructed of 420J2 stainless steel, it is corrosion resistant, an important characteristic for a knife which will be worn close to the body as boot knives are intended to be. For use by combat swimmers or other divers, the Amphibian is available with a diver's sheath designed for wear on the arm or leg.

Overall Length: 7.8 inches
Blade Length: 3.8 inches
Weight: 3.2 ounces
Blade Type: Double-edged Spear Point, partially serrated, blood groove
Crossguard: Double, integral
Grip: Open-tang with polymer insert, serrated near crossguard
Sheath: Leather with boot clip, retention strap
Source: Kershaw Knives, 25300 SW Parkway Ave., Wilsonville, OR 97070, (503) 682-1966, www.kershawknives.com

Kershaw Amphibian Boot Knife

Kershaw Trooper

Kershaw Trooper

The Trooper has a well established reputation as a military close-combat knife, though it is actually a bit large for a boot knife. As a result, I would prefer that it came with a sheath better designed for carrying laced to a soldier's gear. Still, this is a well designed, well balanced, double-edged fighting knife. It is very popular as a military presentation knife – one reason it comes in a fitted presentation case. Rex Applegate was a fan of the Trooper and frequently recommended it to military personnel.

Overall Length: 9.5 inches
Blade Length: 5.3 inches
Weight: 7.8 ounces
Blade Type: Double-edged Spear Point, AUS8A stainless steel
Crossguard: Double, stainless steel
Grip: Ebony, with steel pommel, wrist-thong hole
Sheath: Leather with boot clip
Source: Kershaw Knives, 25300 SW Parkway Ave., Wilsonville, OR 97070, (503) 682-1966, www.kershawknives.com

Mad Dog A.T.A.K. (Advanced Tactical Assault Knife)

If members of the U.S. military special operations community were asked what knife they would choose as their personal combat knife, a substantial number would say a Mad Dog A.T.A.K. Mad Dog knives are very highly thought of among professionals whose combat knives receive hard service. Reports of Mad Dog Knives being used to pry open car doors in Iraq are not unknown, an indicator of their legendary toughness. Kevin McClung has a background which makes him attuned to the needs of military and police special operations personnel and he crafts each knife with the same care as if his own life were dependent upon it.

McClung puts great stress upon the steel used in his knives and selectively tempers them so that they have excellent edge-holding characteristics as well as toughness. I would recommend that anyone interested in understanding the process of knife heat-treating and tempering read McClung's article cited in the Suggested Reading section at the end of this book.

Mad Dog Knives are designed to

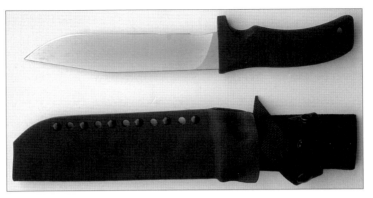

Mad Dog A.T.A.K.

stand up to heat and electrical shock as well as oils, chemicals, blood, saltwater, etc. Along with a full-length tang, the A.T.A.K. incorporates a choil that thickens at the grip for even more durability in hacking. The A.T.A.K. passed rigorous tests carried out by Naval Special Warfare Personnel, but even more importantly has passed the test of use in many of the world's trouble spots. The A.T.A.K. is not fancy and lacks frills, but it is arguably one of the world's very best combat knives. It is quite often the choice for those who must have a knife that absolutely will not fail.

Overall Length: 11.8 inches
Blade Length: 7 inches
Weight: 12.5 ounces
Blade Type: Clip Point, Starrett alloy 49-06, flat ground from .25-inch stock, selectively tempered, hard chromed
Crossguard: Single, integral with grip
Grip: Black glass/epoxy composite, wrist-thong hole, designed to withstand 300 degrees F, 1,000 volts of electricity, etc.
Sheath: Kydex with retention strap
Source: MD Tactical, 3010 W. Orange Ave., Suite 101, Anaheim, CA 92804, (714) 220-0719, www.mdtactical.com

Mad Dog Mirage-X

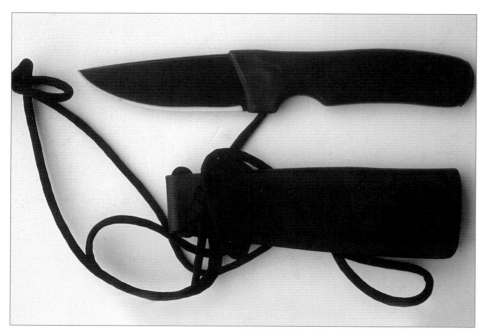

Mad Dog Mirage-X

The Mirage-X series of knives is specifically designed for clandestine operations where a non-metallic knife is needed. In addition to military special operations personnel and intelligence agents, Explosive Ordnance Disposal teams also use these knives, since the Mirage-X has no magnetic signature. The Mirage-X is also safe to use around electricity since it is non-conductive and it does not generate a field in salt water so will not affect field-sensing devices. This knife holds an edge better than virtually any other knife available and can cut glass or shave steel off other knives. It is also completely corrosion-proof. Although other non-metallic knives have been offered, they pale in comparison to the Mirage-X. In addition to the version illustrated, a Mirage-X with a longer 4-inch blade is also available. Because of this knife's special characteristics, it is normally only available to members of military or law enforcement agencies.

Overall Length: 7.5 inches
Blade Length: 3.2 inches
Weight: 4.8 ounces
Blade Type: Single-edged, Alumina ceramic
Crossguard: None
Grip: Elasopolymer
Sheath: Kydex, with neck cord
Source: MD Tactical, 3010 W. Orange Ave., Suite 101, Anaheim, CA 92804, (714) 220-0719, www.mdtactical.com

Mad Dog T.U.S.K. (Tactical Utility Sniper Knife)

Originally designed for U.S. Marine Corps Snipers, the TUSK is intended for heavy duty. The sniper may need a knife to cut trees or brush to build a hide but may also need to force open a door to reach a rooftop or even hack through a wall to enter a barn or in urban combat. The TUSK is sturdy enough to perform these tasks and many more. It incorporates saw teeth that are actually usable and comes with a stone specifically designed to sharpen these teeth. Despite the fact it is built to stand up to hard general usage, the balance and design of the TUSK are such that it can be a devastating close-combat knife if necessary as well.

Overall Length: 15.2 inches
Blade Length: 10 inches
Weight: 23 ounces
Blade Type: Straight Clip, flat ground from .25-inch stock, fully serrated
Crossguard: Single, integral with grip
Grip: Black glass/epoxy composite, wrist-thong holes
Sheath: Kydex with retention strap
Source: MD Tactical, 3010 W. Orange Ave., Suite 101, Anaheim, CA 92804, (714) 220-0719, www.mdtactical.com

Mad Dog T.U.S.K.

Al Mar SERE Operator

Al Mar SERE Operator

The original Al Mar SERE was a heavy-duty folding knife developed for the U.S. Army's Survival, Escape, Resistance, Evasion (SERE) course to train personnel in evading capture or escaping and evading after capture. The fixed-blade SERE remains a good combat escape and evasion or combat knife. One of its most appealing characteristics is that it is quite slim, the total width with scales at the widest point being only half an inch. It is also quite light and very lively in the hand. The tight fit in the sheath combined with the rubber retention ring, plus the various mounting options with straps or laces, allow the SERE Operator to be readily carried upside-down on webbed gear. The SERE Operator would appear to be especially useful in those situations where a light, compact knife which can still function as a fighting knife or utility knife is most desirable (e.g. on an aircrew survival vest).

Overall Length: 10.3 inches
Blade Length: 5 inches
Weight: 6 ounces
Blade Type: Clip Point with saw teeth
Crossguard: Small, double, integral with grip and blade
Grip: Prylon with wrist-thong hole
Sheath: Molded Prylon, with rubber retaining ring, multiple mounting options on belt or gear
Source: Al Mar Knives, P.O. Box 2295, Tualatin, OR 97062, (503) 670-9080, www.almarknives.com

Masters of Defense CQD (Close Quarters Defense) MKV ATAC

The ATAC is misleading on first look as one has a tendency to think it has style over substance. However, as one examines the different features, this impression is quickly proved wrong. A good example is the Side Hilt, which serves multiple purposes: 1) it provides pressure and striking points; 2) it prevents the blade over-penetrating; 3) it acts as a blade catcher; 4) it allows lashing if used as a spear for survival; and 5) it allows use as a prying or puncturing device while protecting the primary point. The Dieter Side Hilt, which takes its name from close-combat expert Duane Dieter, allows greater control of the blade, keeps the thumb from shifting forward, offers additional protection from cuts or slashes from an opponent's blade, and acts as part of the blade's retention system in the sheath.

Among other useful features are a pommel that may be used for hammering or delivering strikes, and a non-conductive grip. The blade incorporates a double edge allowing cuts or slashes in either direction. Lower-blade serrations may be used for sawing, while the pressure plate on the back of the blade allows easy use of the thumb as well as allowing pressure to be applied more easily to the top of the blade

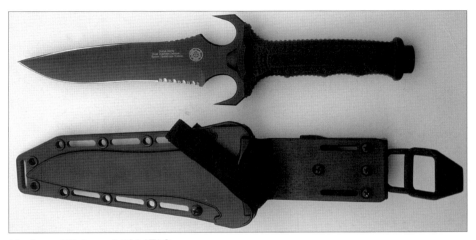

Masters of Defense MKV ATAC

with the palm. The broadening blade allows a wider wound channel and easier retraction after a thrust, while the forward-weight design allows greater force to be applied when hacking.

The ATAK does, indeed, look stylish, but it is also a very well designed special operations knife.

Overall Length: 12.6 inches
Blade Length: 6.8 inches
Weight: 16.2 ounces

Blade Type: Modified Spear Point, serrations, black TiCN-coated
Crossguard: Double, striker hilt
Grip: Glass-impregnated Zytel, finger grooved, textured, wrist-thong hole
Sheath: Polymer with rubber ring and cross strap retention, belt loop and other strap or lacing attachment points
Source: Masters of Defense, 256-A Industrial Park Dr. Waynesville, NC 28786, (828) 452-4158, www.mastersofdefense.com

Mercworx Seraphym

Mercworx Seraphym

allows the blade to be used for thrusts or slashes while using the clenched-fist grip comfortable to many who have not had extensive close-combat training. The small double guard incorporated into the blade helps protect the fingers but also helps keep the Seraphym in position while in use since one problem with some push daggers is a tendency to flip in the hand. The Seraphym is also sturdier than many push daggers which will keep it from damage should it have to be thrust through intervening material. As with all Mercworx blades, the Seraphym combines good workmanship and sturdiness with style.

Overall Length: 5 inches
Blade Length: 3 inches
Weight: 3.8 ounces
Blade Type: Double-edged Spear Point
Crossguard: Double, integral with blade
Grip: T-handled, Micarta
Sheath: Kydex, neck chain or belt loop
Source: Mercworx, 235 Main St., #287, Madison, NJ 07940, (908) 619-1013, www.mercworx.com

This compact push dagger is designed to offer a very effective close-combat weapon that may be easily concealed. As is normal with the push dagger, it

Mercworx Shiva

The Shiva is the Mercworx take on the classic F-S knife, though with improvements. As with the Applegate-Fairbairn, the Shiva incorporates a much thicker, sturdier blade and a grip which will not turn in the hand and which immediately lets one know the orientation of the knife by feel. Constructed of 154Cm polished stainless steel, the Shiva is also quite durable. The knife is hilt-heavy, the type of balance preferred by many with a double-edged fighting knife. In addition to various attachment points, the sheath incorporates a pocket for a sharpening stone or other items. As with most stilettos, the Shiva is intended as a fighting knife rather than a combat/utility knife; however, it is sturdy enough that it should stand up to hard usage. I have always been a fan of the basic F-S stiletto design and have used many variations, but I find that the Shiva is my favorite.

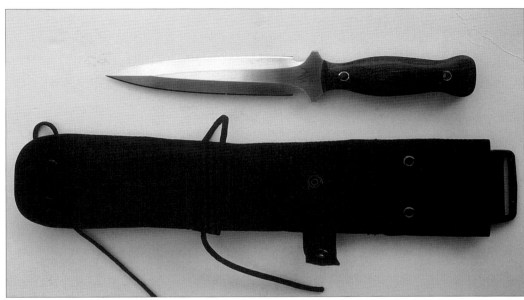

Mercworx Shiva

Overall Length: 11 inches
Blade Length: 6.5 inches
Weight: 12.4 ounces
Blade Type: Double-edged Spear Point
Crossguard: Double, integral with blade

Grip: Micarta, with wrist-thong hole
Sheath: Ballistic nylon with loops and lacing holes for various carry modes
Source: Mercworx, 235 Main St., #287, Madison, NJ 07940, (908) 619-1013, www.mercworx.com

Mercworx Sniper

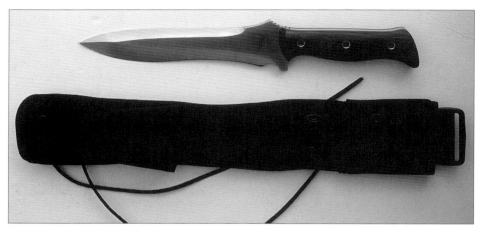

Mercworx Sniper

The rationale for and mission of a specialized knife for snipers has been discussed under the entry for Mad Dog's TUSK. The Sniper takes a somewhat different approach; while the Sniper is designed to be tough enough to use for hacking and chopping, it is also designed to serve as a close-combat knife as well. Mercworx does a substantial amount of business with contract special ops advisors in Africa where the Sniper has proven quite popular as an all-round

combat knife as well as a specialized blade for snipers. Note, too, that a larger version, designated the Equatorian, is available from Mercworx as well. Though perhaps an oversimplification, it might be said that the Mad Dog TUSK is designed primarily to serve as a heavy-duty combat/utility knife and secondarily as a close-combat knife, while the Sniper is intended to serve primarily as a close-combat knife and secondarily as a combat/utility knife. By increasing its

usable edge surface area, the re-curved blade gives the Sniper substantial chopping ability even though its blade is only 7.5 inches in length. Based on my own experiences training Third World military units, the Sniper's stylish appearance may lend a certain panache to advisors using it as well. Note, too, that the Sniper is available with another grip style known as the "Chili Pepper" grip because of its appearance. This grip is quite ergonomic and fills the hand well when using the Sniper for chopping. I think the larger Equatorian with the Chili Grip should make quite an impressive chopping knife.

Overall Length: 13 inches
Blade Length: 7.5 inches
Weight: 16.6 ounces
Blade Type: Double-edged, re-curved
Crossguard: Double, integral with blade, upper serrated as a thumb rest
Grip: Micarta with three wrist-thong/lanyard holes
Sheath: Ballistic nylon with loops and lacing holes for various carry modes
Source: Mercworx, 235 Main St., #287, Madison, NJ 07940, (908) 619-1013, www.mercworx.com

Mission Knives MPS (Multi-Purpose Survival)

Mission Knives specializes in producing titanium knives that are quite popular with Explosive Ordnance Disposal personnel because they are non-magnetic. Titanium knives are also very tough and corrosion-resistant as well as light. As a result, they are popular with combat swimmer units. The MPS is designed as an aircrew survival knife, though it can perform other combat tasks well. In fact, its dimensions are such that it will fit in the U.S. pilot's survival vest sheath. It has serrations atop the blade designed to act as a thumb rest or point for applying pressure with the palm. The only real downside to Mission or other titanium knives is that it is hard to get them to take and hold an edge, though with the proper diamond sharpener one can do an acceptable job.

Mission Knives MPS

Overall Length: 9.8 inches
Blade Length: 4.7 inches
Weight: 5.2 ounces
Blade Type: Clip Point, partially serrated
Crossguard: Single, lower, integral with blade and grip
Grip: One piece with blade, skeletonized, and wrist-thong hole

Sheath: Kydex with single retention strap, lacing holes and strap loops for various attachment methods
Source: Mission Knives and Tools Inc., P.O. Box 17247, Anaheim, CA 92817, (714) 777 7881, www.missionknives.com

MOD Survival Knife

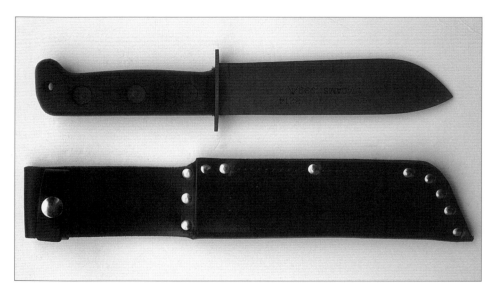

MOD Survival Knife

This heavy-duty knife has been issued to the British RAF, Navy and Army for four decades and has served well as its longevity indicates. This is not a good close-combat knife as it is heavy and not at all lively in the hand. Its forté is chopping, but the bulky wooden grip panels, which are not well fitted, have a tendency to cause blisters if the knife is used extensively. On the positive side, this knife will stand up to hard usage and is certainly tougher than many general-issue knives which tend to be designed as fighting knives first and survival/combat knives second. Since most military combat knives are used far more often for utility purposes, the MOD knife is actually more practical than many other general issue military knives. It probably makes sense to supplement it with a good multi-tool and, if in an infantry unit, perhaps a folding close-combat knife.

Overall Length: 12.3 inches
Blade Length: 7 inches
Weight: 18.8 ounces
Blade Type: Drop Point with NATO stores code, Parkerized
Crossguard: Double
Grip: Wood panels, with wrist-thong hole
Sheath: Leather with snap retaining strap
Source: Wilkinson, Hopkinson's, J. Adams and possibly other Sheffield makers.

No Lie Blade Training Knife

This is a very cleverly designed training knife. The felt, which is affixed to the blade, is designed to have lipstick rubbed onto it so that any strikes on a training partner can be quickly spotted. The knife is also provided with a detailed training chart that shows vulnerable points for cuts, slashes and thrusts. Overall, this is quite a practical training system which would be useful for military units or others who use the blade in close combat as well as for law enforcement or security personnel to train them in defense against the blade.

Overall Length: 11.5 inches
Blade Length: 7 inches
Weight: 5.2 ounces
Blade Type: Aluminum, training
  with felt edges for marking
Crossguard: None
Grip: Cord wrapped
Sheath: Polymer and ballistic nylon
Source: No Lie Blades,
  www.nolieblades.com

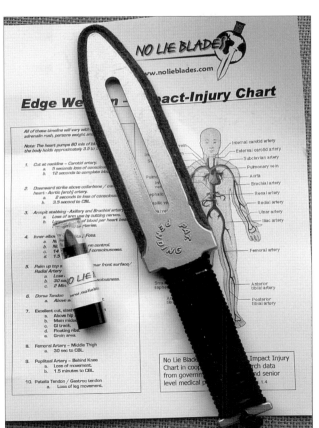

No Lie Blades Training Knife

Ontario Knife Company RTAK

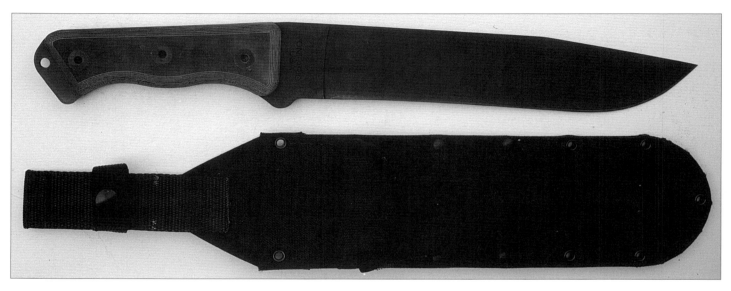

The RTAK was designed by the survival training team at Randall's Adventure and Training as a heavy-duty bush knife. Intended to offer a compromise between a heavy-duty knife and a machete, the RTAK is a useful combat knife for troops likely to be deployed in the jungle or forest. It would also make a good choice as a survival kit knife for bush pilots. Though primarily a heavy-duty combat utility knife, the RTAK is well balanced and would make a fearsome close-combat weapon as well.

Overall Length: 17.1 inches
Blade Length: 10 inches
Weight: 22 ounces
Blade Type: Clip Point
Crossguard: Single, integral with blade
Grip: Linen Micarta with extended tang and lanyard/wrist-thong hole

Ontario Knife Company RTAK

Sheath: Ballistic nylon with accessory pocket, single retention strap, multiple attachment points
Source: Ontario Knife Company, P.O. Box 145, Franklinville, NY 14737, (716) 676-5527, www.ontarioknife.com

Puma Tac 1

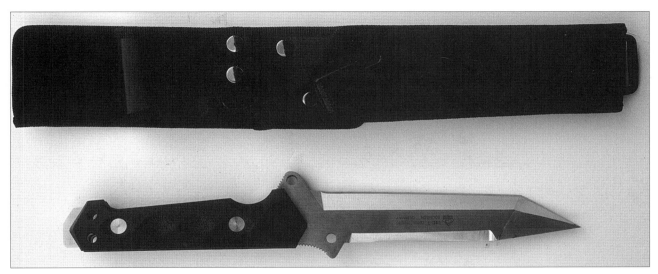

The Tac 1 is an interesting rather high-tech military knife that has seen use with German military units. Its single beveled edge is somewhat uncommon, but does ease sharpening to some extent. The knife is constructed of stainless steel and has a well designed blade for penetrating, slashing or cutting, and chopping. On the back of the blade is a chopping edge. The grip is really quite ergonomic and makes the knife feel quite lively in the hand. As with most Puma knives, the Tac 1 offers sound design and good quality at a reasonable price.

Overall Length: 12.2 inches
Blade Length: 6 inches
Weight: 10.8 ounces
Blade Type: Tanto, single beveled edge, chopping edge on back of blade
Crossguard: Double, integral with blade, with lashing holes

Grip: ABS, with textured finger grooves, extended tang, double wrist-thong- or lashing holes
Sheath: Ballistic nylon and leather, with D-ring for lashing, buckle retaining strap
Source: Puma-Werke, Lauterjung & Sohn GmbH & Co. KG, Schneidwaren-Manufactur, 42699 Solingen, Germany.

Randall Model 2 Fighting Stiletto

Randall Model 2 Fighting Stiletto

Randall knives have established a reputation for quality with U.S. combat troops in every war since the Second World War, many having gone to war with the sons and grandsons of their original owners. The Model 2 is one of the designs which was produced in the Second World War and has remained popular with those who like a combat stiletto. Randall offered the Model 2 as an improvement on the Fairbairn-Sykes knife, one that had a stronger blade and a hilt less likely to roll in the hands. The version illustrated is fabricated of stainless steel, though Randalls are also offered in high-carbon tool steel. As is normally the case, tool steel will take and hold an edge better than stainless, but stainless offers greater corrosion resistance. Randall's reputation for excellence has now lasted for more than sixty years. Throughout the many conflicts in which U.S. soldiers have been involved during that period, the Randall has remained one of the infantryman's most coveted possessions – justifiably so.

Overall Length: 11.6 inches
Blade Length: 7 inches
Weight: 9 ounces
Blade Type: Double-edged Spear Point
Crossguard: Double, brass
Grip: Contoured black Micarta with wrist-thong hole, aluminum butt cap
Sheath: Leather with retention strap and sharpening-stone pocket
Source: Randall Made Knives; P.O. Box 1988, Orlando, FL 32802, (407) 855-8075, www.randallknives.com

Randall Model 14 Attack

The Model 14 originated as the result of a U.S. Marine Corps request for a combat survival knife in 1954. The model shown with 7.5-inch blade was intended for ground troops while the 5.5-inch bladed model, cataloged by Randall as the Model 15 Airman, was intended for aircrew. From Vietnam through the present, the Model 14 has remained one of the most popular Randalls with U.S. military personnel who value its ability to serve as a heavy-duty utility blade as well as a close-combat weapon. For those who do not like the finger groove grips, the Model 14 is available with other grips. Also, note that Model 14s without saw teeth normally have a clipped point blade. I own three Randalls, all of which I have used extensively, but the Model 14 is the one that I have carried the most often. It has always performed well.

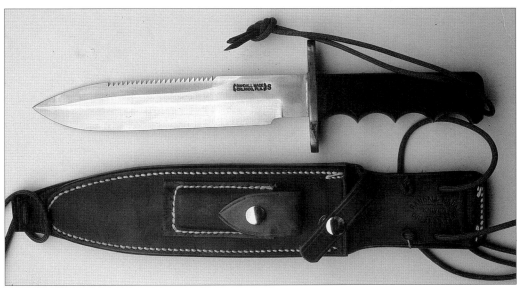

Randall Model 14 Attack

Overall Length: 12 inches
Blade Length: 7.5 inches
Weight: 15 ounces
Blade Type: Drop Point with saw teeth
Crossguard: Double, brass
Grip: Black Micarta with finger grooves and wrist-thong hole

Sheath: Leather with retention strap, lashing holes and sharpening-stone pocket
Source: Randall Made Knives; P.O. Box 1988, Orlando, FL 32802, (407) 855-8075, www.randallknives.com

Randall Model 18 Attack-Survival

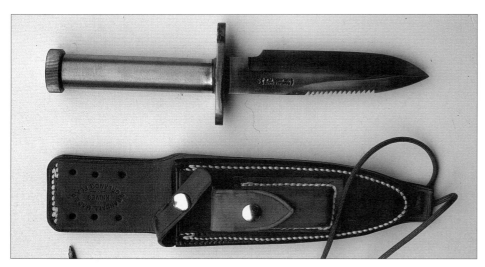

Randall Model 18 Attack-Survival

There are two schools of thought about hollow-handled survival knives; one group feels that the hollow handle weakens the knife, especially since it precludes a full-length tang; others are willing to sacrifice a bit of strength for the benefit of the handle storage. I have used Randall Model 18s and other hollow-handled combat knives for many years and have never seen a Randall Model 18's blade separate from its handle, even when the knife received rough usage. I like the idea of the storage space in the handle and believe that these knives fill a useful niche.

Overall Length: 10.5 inches
Blade Length: 5.5 inches
Weight: 13.4 ounces
Blade Type: Drop Point with saw teeth
Crossguard: Double, brass, with lashing holes
Grip: Stainless steel, tubular (hollow), brass screw cap
Sheath: Leather with retention strap, lashing holes, and sharpening-stone pocket
Source: Randall Made Knives; P.O. Box 1988, Orlando, FL 32802, (407) 855-8075, www.randallknives.com

The Attack-Survival, as its name implies, was intended as a combat knife that could serve in close combat as well as survival. Its hollow handle is designed to carry critical survival items such as water purification tablets, fishing line, fishing hooks, waterproof matches, etc. It is also designed so that the hollow handle can be placed over a pole, then lashed down using the two holes in the crossguard to create a spear. I used a 7.5-inch Model 18 for many years but then switched to the 5.5-inch model as it carried a bit easier when riding in vehicles or helicopters. Many users wrap fishing line around the smooth handle to create a surer grip and to carry the line without taking up room in the handle or elsewhere in the gear. More recent Model 18s are available with knurled grips if so desired.

Chris Reeve Green Beret

Developed for the U.S. Army Special Forces which designates this as the "Yarborough" knife and presents it to each graduate of the Special Forces Qualification Course, the Green Beret is a heavy-duty combat knife. The finger-grooved Grip is very comfortable, while the knife balances well. Heavy enough for chopping, it remains lively enough for close combat. The sharpening-stone or utility pocket on the front of the sheath is large enough to accommodate other gear or even a folding knife or multi-tool. Overall, this is quite a good special operations knife, handsome enough in a deadly sort of way to fit its mission as a presentation piece, but tough enough and utilitarian enough to serve with those graduates of the Q-Course throughout their spec ops careers.

Chris Reeve Green Beret

Overall Length: 12.4 inches
Blade Length: 7 inches
Weight: 11.6 ounces
Blade Type: Drop Point, partially serrated, stainless steel with KG Gun-Kote finish
Crossguard: Double, integral with blade

Grip: Black canvas Micarta, full tang with wrist-thong hole
Sheath: Green ballistic nylon with various mounting points, sharpening-stone pocket

Source: Chris Reeve Knives, 11624 W. President Drive, #B, Boise, ID 83713, (208) 375-0367, www.chrisreeve.com

Chris Reeve Nronka

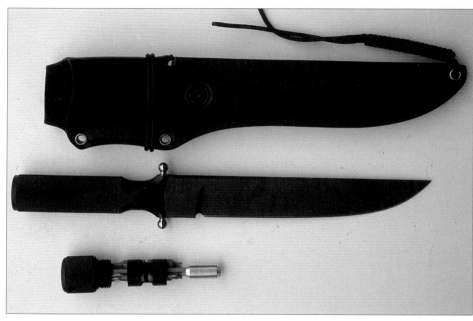

Chris Reeve Nronka

Chris Reeve is best known for his hollow-handled knives that are machined from one billet of steel, thus eliminating the problem of a short tang, which weakens some hollow-handled designs. Each hollow-handled knife has a butt cap of 6061 aluminum and a Neoprene O-ring for moisture proofing. Unlike many hollow-handled knives, however, the Nronka is designed to contain specific items in the handle. Based on Chris Reeve's own experiences with motorcycles, the Nronka contains a cleverly designed screwdriver kit in the handle. This would, of course, be useful for anyone who uses mechanical equipment away from civilization. Those who ride trail bikes, all-terrain vehicles, sport utility vehicles, etc. might all find this an excellent utility knife and tool. For military personnel who might have to repair equipment as well – those assigned to Fast Attack Vehicles for example – the Nronka offers a tough combat utility knife, which may also be used to make equipment repairs. I have been impressed with every Chris Reeve knife I have used, and the Nronka is no exception.

Overall Length: 12.5 inches
Blade Length: 7.5 inches
Weight: 17.4 ounces
Blade Type: Straight Clip, A2 tool steel
Crossguard: Double, titanium, "bedpost" finials
Grip: Tubular steel, knurled, hollow
Sheath: Leather soaked in polyurethane for water resistance
Source: Chris Reeve Knives, 11624 W. President Drive, #B, Boise, ID 83713,

Russian Ballistic Knife

This knife shows how the Russian Special Forces are just as fascinated with gadgets as their Western counterparts. Although this knife was originally developed for the Soviet Spetsnaz, it was later copied in the USA. I have included it as a curiosity, but I do not really consider it a viable combat knife. Although the idea of a knife that fires its blade into an opponent some distance away may seem appealing, a suppressed firearm would actually work more effectively. Additionally, this knife is complicated and difficult to load and operate safely. I think that this knife would be more likely to inflict casualties on those using it than on an enemy!

Overall Length: 13.4 inches (with safety shield in place)
Blade Length: 4 inches
Weight: 9.4 ounces
Blade Type: Spear Point
Crossguard: None, though a portion of the spring-loaded launcher can function as a crossguard
Grip: Steel, tubular, knurled
Sheath: None, but a protective shield covers the blade
Source: Soviet/Russian State Arsenals

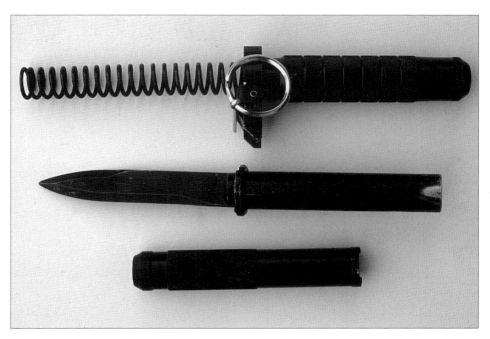

Russian Ballistic Knife

SOG Scuba/Demo

SOG Scuba/Demo

SOG Knives took its name from the original knife it produced, a copy of the U.S. Army Special Forces SOG (Special Operations Group) knife of the Vietnam era. Though SOG has expanded its line with many quality knives, it still offers three of the "SOG" knives. This one, the Scuba/Demo is based on a knife produced in small numbers for combat swimmer operations along the North Vietnamese Coast. The knife itself is very handsome and has been used as a presentation piece by some military units, but it is also a quite functional combat knife. Relatively heavy and with usable saw teeth, the Scuba/Demo can pry, chop, saw, or perform other utility tasks. It is also well balanced enough to serve as a close-combat knife. SOG knives offer good quality, affordable production knives that will stand up to combat usage.

Overall Length: 12.3 inches
Blade Length: 7.3 inches
Weight: 12.8 ounces
Blade Type: Drop Point, with serrations, AUS 8 stainless steel
Crossguard: Double, brass
Grip: Epoxied leather washers with brass pommel cap, wrist-thong hole and wrist thong
Sheath: Leather with sharpening-stone pocket and stone, snap retention strap
Source: SOG, 6521 212th St, SW, Lynnwood, WA 98036, (425) 771-6230, www.sogknives.com

SOG SEAL 2000

While the Scuba/Demo harks back to a classic combat swimmer knife of the Vietnam era, the SEAL 2000 was designed for U.S. government testing for the Navy's SEALs. In tests which included tip breaking strength, blade breaking toughness, sharpness and edge retention, handle twist-off limits, two-week saltwater immersion tests, gasoline and acetylene-torch resistance, chopping, hammering, prying, penetration, cutting of six different types of rope and nylon line, low noise and reflectivity evaluation, plus overall ergonomics and handling, the SEAL 2000 received very high marks. The SEAL 2000 is sturdy enough as one might expect from the tests it was designed to undergo, yet it remains handy. For close combat, it is not as lively in the hand as some other knives, but it will be used far more often as a general combat/ utility knife, and it can certainly do the job should it be used as a fighting knife. The scabbard is well designed for military users as well since it allows upside-down carry or strapping to the leg when swimming. Designed for a tough job, this is a tough knife.

SOG SEAL 2000

Overall Length: 12.3 inches
Blade Length: 7 inches
Weight: 12.8 ounces
Blade Type: Clip Point, partially serrated, AUS6 powder-coated stainless steel
Crossguard: Single, integral with grip
Grip: Zytel, checkered, with finger grooves and wrist-thong hole

Sheath: Kydex, friction and strap retention, multiple mounting systems
Source: SOG, 6521 212th St, SW, Lynnwood, WA 98036, (425) 771-6230, www.sogknives.com

SOG X-42 Recondo

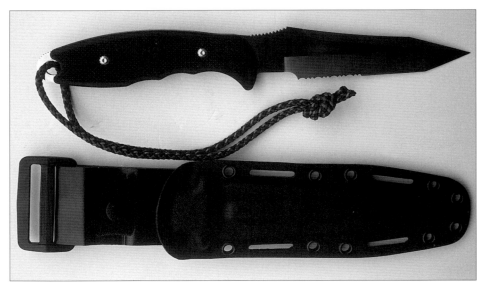

SOG X-42 Recondo

reflective blade. I like the Recondo quite a bit and find it one of the better production light combat knives.

Overall Length: 10.5 inches
Blade Length: 5.3 inches
Weight: 6.3 ounces
Blade Type: Semi-Tanto, partially serrated, thumb grooves on back
Crossguard: Single, integral with grip
Grip: Zytel, finger-grooved, checkered, wrist-thong hole
Sheath: Kydex with friction and strap retention, multiple mounting systems
Source: SOG, 6521 212th St, SW, Lynnwood, WA 98036, (425) 771-6230, www.sogknives.com

The Recondo is lighter than many of SOG's fixed-blade knives but is still quite versatile as a combat knife. Light enough to be carried on an aircrewman's survival vest, the Recondo has good balance, and a penetrating point and edges for slashing or cutting maneuvers; hence, it is a functional close-combat knife. Designed by Spencer Frazier, the Recondo is fabricated of BG-42 steel, a steel used in jet-engine parts and renowned for its edge-holding ability. The X-42 Recondo is also available with a black TiNi hard coating for units which need a non-

Spyderco Bob Lum Tanto

Of Spyderco's fixed-blade knives, this is my favorite. Though quite compact, the Bob Lum Tanto is well designed for close combat and has the advantage of good penetrating ability granted by the Tanto blade. For a soldier going against an opponent who might be wearing substantial equipment, this is an important consideration. The tip has a Hamaguri (Appleseed) grind for added strength, while a swedge has been ground from the spine to lower weight. This swedge also allows the back of the blade to be used for light chopping. Fabricated of AUS-8 stainless steel, the Bob Lum Tanto will also be durable. This is a very nice compact fighting knife.

Overall Length: 8.4 inches
Blade Length: 4.2 inches
Blade Type: Tanto
Crossguard: Double, integral with blade
Grip: Black linen Micarta
Sheath: Leather, friction retention
Source: Spyderco, Inc., 820 Spyderco Way, Golden, CO 80403, (303) 279-8383, www.spyderco.com

Spyderco Bob Lum Tanto

Timberline Aviator

Timberline Aviator

This Vaughan Neeley-designed pilot survival knife is an interesting take on that mission since it employs a design best suited for close combat rather than general combat/utility usage. Still, the Aviator's blade is tough and should perform most light chores required of an aviator's knife. The sheath is well designed for mounting in various ways about the person, and the knife is compact and light, both useful features in an aviator's survival knife.

Overall Length: 8.8 inches
Blade Length: 3.4 inches
Weight: 7.8 ounces
Blade Type: Chisel-ground Tanto
Crossguard: Integral with grip
Grip: Kraton with wrist-thong hole
Sheath: Kydex, with multiple mounting points, friction and strap retention
Source: Timberline Knives, P.O. Box 600, Getzville, NY 14068-0600, (716) 877-2200, www.timberlineknives.com

Timberline Zambezi

This Greg Lightfoot design is very handsome and is also quite functional. Well balanced for utility usage, the Zambezi is also lively enough in the hands for close combat. The deeply serrated thumb ramp allows good control of the blade as well as offering a point for pressure with the thumb or palm, especially when wearing gloves. Once one becomes used to the button release mechanism, it is quite easy to carry the knife securely without use of a retention strap, yet gain access to the knife quickly. The Zambezi is a good medium-duty combat knife, which can perform utility tasks or serve as a fighting knife.

Overall Length: 11.8 inches
Blade Length: 6 inches
Weight: 10.8 inches
Blade Type: Clip Point, swedge-ground, partially serrated, non-glare powder coating
Crossguard: None
Grip: Contoured olive Zytel with Kraton slip-resistant ribs, wrist-thong hole

Timberline Zambezi

Sheath: Kydex with ballistic nylon, friction and button lock retention, multiple mounting points

Source: Timberline Knives, P.O. Box 600, Getzville, NY 14068-0600, (716) 877-2200, www.timberlineknives.com

TOPS Knives Armageddon

TOPS Armageddon

TOPS designs and builds its knives based heavily on the experiences of its advisory staff of military- and law-enforcement professionals. As a result, TOPS knives are designed to stand up to tough usage, and the Armageddon is one of the toughest. This is a heavy-duty utility knife of the type I previously discussed for use by snipers. It is also a good choice for military personnel or outdoorsmen who operate in heavy brush or jungle and may need a heavy knife for hacking. These heavy-duty hacking or chopping knives, if well balanced and well designed, can also make fearsome close-combat weapons; this is the case with the Armageddon which is very lively in the hands. The sheath is also quite useful as it allows carry in various ways on webbed gear or pack and also incorporates a sizable pocket for gear, folding knife, etc. I like the Armageddon quite a bit and consider it a real bargain in heavy-duty combat knives.

Overall Length: 16.5 inches
Blade Length: 10.6 inches
Weight: 22.2 ounces
Blade Type: Clip Point, black traction coating
Crossguard: Single, integral with blade
Grip: Linen Micarta, partially finger-grooved, extended tang with double wrist-thong- or lashing holes
Sheath: Ballistic nylon, with Kydex liner, two retention straps, multiple mounting points, sharpening stone- or utility pocket
Source: TOPS Knives, P.O. Box 2544, Idaho Falls, ID 83403, (208) 542-0113, www.topsknives.com

TOPS Knives BEST (Black Eagle Strike Team)

Although I like every TOPS knife I have tried, the BEST is my favorite. I especially like the combination of the pry-bar hilt and the chopping edge on the spine. Both of these features are useful in a combat knife and protect the point and primary edge from hard usage. Although only rarely is a combat/survival knife employed as a spear for fishing, the lashing holes on the crossguard are useful should it prove desirable to lash the blade to a spear shaft. The use of 154 CM CRYO treated steel also ensures good edge-retention. Although the camouflage finish isn't really necessary, I have to admit I like it and feel it gives the BEST a certain style. The standard black traction coating is, however, quite functional. Though a heavy knife, the balance of the BEST is still good enough such that it can serve in close combat if necessary. As with all TOPS knives, this one offers extreme value-for-money. An interesting aspect of TOPS knives is that the company's management seeks input from members of the military and police special operations community and often develops mission-specific knives for a small group. These knives, then, frequently enter production. As a result,

TOPS BEST

I recommend visiting the company website to look at the wide variety of knives available. It is very likely that one to fit most combat needs will be available.

Overall Length: 11.5 inches
Blade Length: 6.5 inches
Weight: 14.8 ounces
Blade Type: Clip Point, with chopping edge on the spine, camouflage finish

Crossguard: Double, integral with blade, two lashing holes
Grip: Linen Micarta, with extended tang which can act as a pry bar or screwdriver
Sheath: Kydex, friction and rubber ring retention; multiple mounting points
Source: TOPS Knives, P.O. Box 2544, Idaho Falls, ID 83403, (208) 542-0113, www.topsknives.com

TOPS Knives Hawk Recon

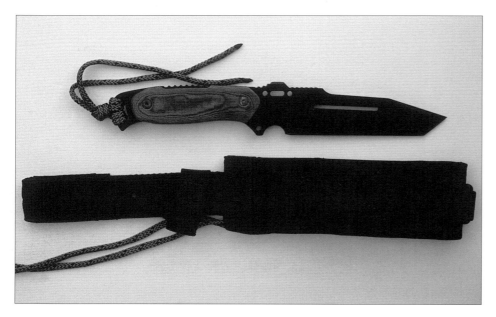

The Hawk Recon is more compact than some of the other TOPS knives I have already discussed, but it is still a heavy-duty combat knife. The stepped spine has an interesting appearance, but it is also quite functional in that it allows use of the thumb readily and also the application of pressure with the palm or heel of the hand. The Tanto Point offers good penetration yet is thick enough such that it will not break easily. The Hawk Recon balances well and the ergonomic grip allows multiple hand positions to make this a good close-combat knife.

Overall Length: 11.3 inches
Blade Length: 5.5 inches
Weight: 13.4 ounces
Blade Type: Tanto with finger recess at the choil, and stepped spine for thumb rest
Crossguard: Single, integral with blade, lashing holes incorporated
Grip: Linen Micarta, extended tang with wrist-thong slot
Sheath: Ballistic nylon with Kydex insert, multiple mounting points, single retention strap, large utility/sharpening stone pocket
Source: TOPS Knives, P.O. Box 2544, Idaho Falls, ID 83403, (208) 542-0113, www.topsknives.com

United Cutlery Elite Forces Tactical Knife

This basic skeletonized knife offers a simple, inexpensive close-combat knife for those who want a knife that is easily replaced if lost or left behind. Its Tanto blade offers the ability to penetrate well, while its edge allows slashes and cuts, and its pommel can be used to deliver blows as well. Additionally, the grip lends itself to alternative holds. On the other hand, the skeletonized slim grip is very uncomfortable if used for any task that requires exerting force. The sheath with its spring stud retention system is quite clever and efficient.

Overall Length: 8.6 inches
Blade Length: 4.4 inches
Weight: 4.6 ounces
Blade Type: Tanto, partially serrated
Crossguard: None
Grip: One-piece 420 J2 stainless steel, blackened, with pry bar/screwdriver pommel
Sheath: Molded, with spring stud retention, multiple mounting points
Source: United Cutlery Corporation, 1425 United Blvd., Sevierville, TN 37876, (865) 428-2532, www.unitedcutlery.com

United Cutlery Elite Forces Tactical Knife

Wilkinson Third Pattern Fairbairn-Sykes Commando Dagger

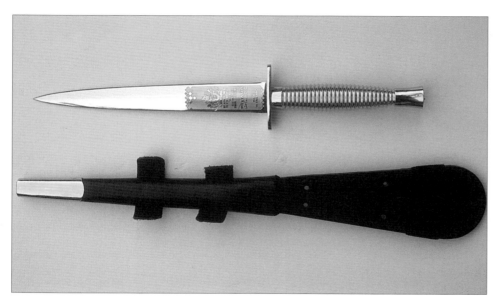

Wilkinson Third Pattern Fairbairn-Sykes Commando Dagger

the belt or sewn to the trouser-leg or inside a cargo pocket, as was the practice with Second World War Commandos. Though the design is more than six decades old, the F-S remains such an icon as a fighting knife that I am very glad it is still available for those who like its classic design.

Overall Length: 11.2 inches
Blade Length: 6.8 inches
Weight: 9.6 ounces
Blade Type: Double-edged Spear Point
Crossguard: Double
Grip: Coke-bottle, ribbed
Sheath: Leather with elastic retention strap, double "ears" for sewing to clothing
Source: Wilkinson Sword Company, US Distributor: ESA, 843 E. 5th, Marysville, OH 43040-1701, (937) 644-2170, www.wilkinson-sword.com

Based on the largest production version of the F-S knife, this model in stainless steel is much more practical as a combat knife for corrosive environments than the traditional steel F-S. However, care will have to be taken to hone and keep a good edge if using this knife for combat. The elastic retention strap used on the original Third Pattern F-S is retained, though this is not really a good retention system and has a tendency to break eventually. As a result, with this sheath, the knife can only be worn on

Benchmade Bali-Song

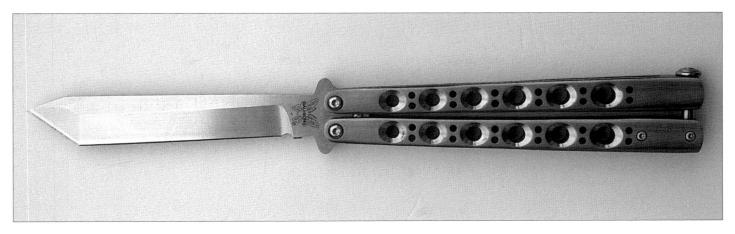

The classic butterfly action is very fast and when in the open position very secure. Many martial-arts techniques are specifically designed for use of the butterfly knife and employ the motions of flipping the knife open as a distraction or prelude to a slash or thrust. This version with the Tanto tip and sharp edge allows a wide variety of close-combat techniques. I am especially fond of Benchmade Bali-Songs, to the extent that I have been using them for twenty years.

Closed Length: 5.2 inches
Open Length: 9.5 inches
Blade Length and Type: 4 inches; Tanto
Weight: 4.1 ounces
Grip: Skeletonized cast titanium with spring latch
Lock: Butterfly
Source: Benchmade Knife Company, 300 Beavercreek Rd., Oregon City, OR 97046, (503) 655-6223, www.benchmade.com

Benchmade Bali-Song

Benchmade Bali-Song Trainer

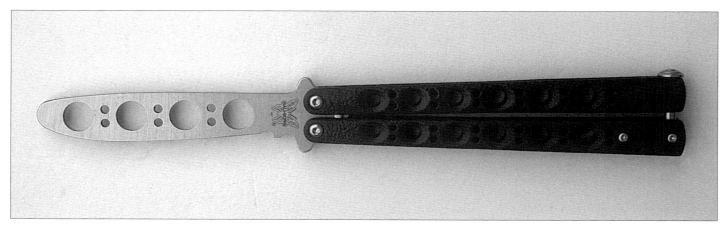

Training is extremely important with the close-combat knife, especially so with the Bali-Song, which can be quite dangerous for its user, if he or she is unskilled in manipulating it; hence the Bali-Song training knife is particularly valuable. Not only can one train against a live opponent safely with it, but one can also work on rapid manipulation of the trainer to hone his or her deployment skills with the sharpened Bali-Song.

Closed Length: 5.2 inches
Open Length: 9 inches
Blade Length and Type: 3.7 inches, blunt, skeletonized training blade
Weight: 4.4 ounces
Grip: Skeletonized titanium, red, with spring latch
Lock: Butterfly
Source: Benchmade Knife Company, 300 Beavercreek Rd., Oregon City, OR 97046, (503) 655-6223, www.benchmade.com

Benchmade Bali-Song Trainer

Benchmade Griptilion

This Mel Pardue design combines many desirable features that make the Griptilion one of the stars of the Benchmade line. This knife is smooth opening and sure locking. It is compact and easy to carry with a button-release lock that keeps one's fingers from under the blade during release. The dual stud allows ease of operation with either hand, and the clip is reversible. The Griptilion also has a very ergonomic grip. As with all Benchmade knives, this one offers excellent value and durability.

Closed Length: 4.5 inches
Open Length: 8 inches
Blade Length and Type: 3.5 inches, modified Drop Point, with dual opening stud
Weight: 3.3 ounces
Grip: Glass-fill Noryl, checkered, with pocket clip
Lock: Axis lock
Source: Benchmade Knife Company, 300 Beavercreek Rd., Oregon City, OR 97046, (503) 655-6223, www.benchmade.com

Benchmade Griptillion

Benchmade Pardue Axis Tanto

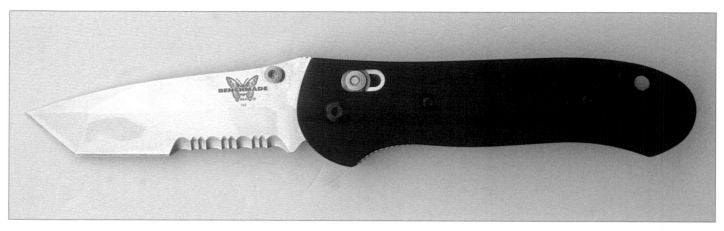

Another Mel Pardue design, the Axis Tanto has a blade of 154CM stainless steel granting corrosion resistance. The Tanto blade allows good penetration for close combat, which combined with the sure Axis lock and the ease of opening make this a lot of close-combat knife for its size.

Closed Length: 4.4 inches
Open Length: 7.6 inches
Blade Length and Type: 3.3 inches, Tanto, partially serrated, with dual opening stud
Weight: 3.8 ounces
Grip: Black G10 scales, ribbed, with pocket clip
Lock: Axis lock
Source: Benchmade Knife Company, 300 Beavercreek Rd., Oregon City, OR 97046, (503) 655-6223, www.benchmade.com

Benchmade Pardue Axis Tanto

Benchmade Stryker Law Enforcement Trainer

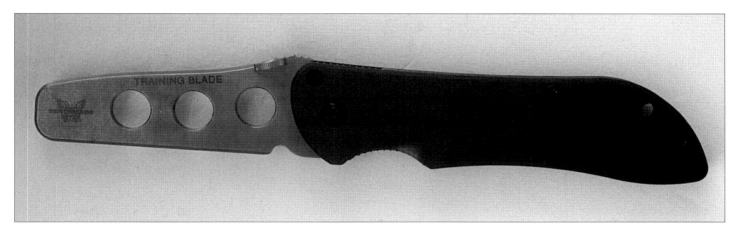

For law enforcement or military users, Benchmade offers a complete line of orange-gripped, blunt-bladed training knives. Since these knives duplicate the feel and opening style of the service versions, they allow very realistic training. It is advisable that any unit that issues a Benchmade knife also purchases the appropriate training knife as well.

Closed Length: 4.7 inches
Open Length: 7.3 inches
Blade Length and Type: 3 inches, blunt training blade with spine-mounted dual opening stud
Weight: 3.8 ounces
Grip: Orange, G10 scales
Lock: Liner lock
Source: Benchmade Knife Company, 300 Beavercreek Rd., Oregon City, OR 97046, (503) 655-6223, www.benchmade.com

Benchmade Stryker Law Enforcement Trainer

Buck Striker Tactical

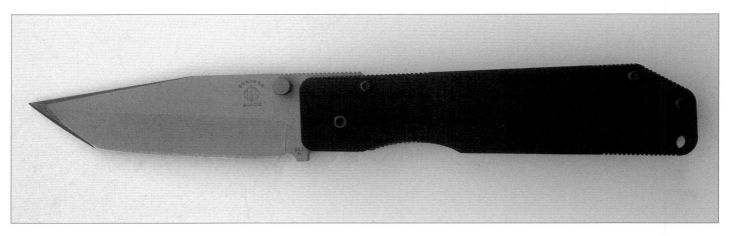

This big, heavy-duty folder is designed for hard usage by military or police personnel. The thick Tanto blade allows puncturing with confidence that the blade will not break. The use of ATS-34 steel aids corrosion resistance while the matte finish keeps the blade non-reflective. Buck Knives helped pioneer sturdy folders for hunters so the Striker Tactical is a logical extension for combat usage.

Closed Length: 5.4 inches
Open Length: 9.3 inches
Blade Length and Type: 4 inches with opening stud and spine serrations
Weight: 5.8 ounces
Grip: G10, with pocket clip and lanyard hole
Lock: Liner
Source: Buck Knives Inc., 1900 Weld Blvd., El Cajon, CA 92020, (619) 449-1100, www.buckknives.com

Buck Striker Tactical

Cold Steel Recon 1 Tanto

The Recon Tanto series are designed as heavy-duty folders. Available with Clip Point, Spear Point or Tanto Point blades fabricated from AUS 8A stainless steel and Teflon-coated, these are designed for long and hard usage. The button blade release is well located for ease of operation whilst exhibiting little chance of the blade being released inadvertently. I like the Recon 1 well enough that I have two – the Tanto version and the Clip Point version. This is a sturdy, versatile knife well worth its price.

Closed Length: 5.3 inches
Open Length: 9.2 inches
Blade Length and Type: 4 inches, Tanto, partially serrated, dual opening disc on spine
Weight: 5.6 ounces
Grip: Zytel with pocket clip
Lock: Ultra Lock pin lock
Source: Cold Steel Inc., 3036-A Seaborg Ave., Ventura, CA 93003, (805) 650-8481, www.coldsteel.com

Cold Steel Recon 1 Tanto

Cold Steel Ti-Lite

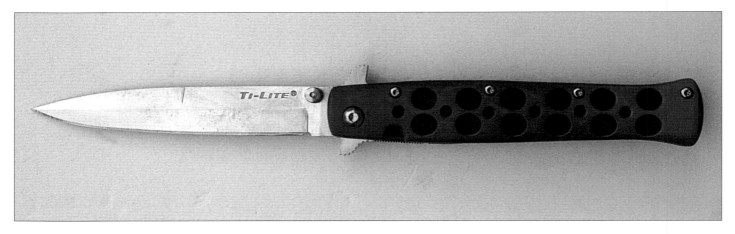

The Ti-Lite is a high-quality, sturdy version of the classic stiletto. I have always thought this design rather elegant and like the fact that Cold Steel offers it in a practical close-combat knife of AUS 8A stainless steel fabrication with a sturdy lock. In addition to classic lines, this knife also offers a well balanced close-combat knife with a blade designed for thrusting or cutting and slashing in either direction.

Closed Length: 5 inches
Open Length: 8.8 inches
Blade Length and Type: 4 inch Spear Point with opening stud, integral double guard
Weight: 4.6 ounces
Grip: Titanium, skeletonized, with pocket clip
Lock: Liner
Source: Cold Steel Inc., 3036-A Seaborg Ave., Ventura, CA 93003, (805) 650-8481, www.coldsteel.com

Cold Steel Ti-Lite

Colt Police Task Force

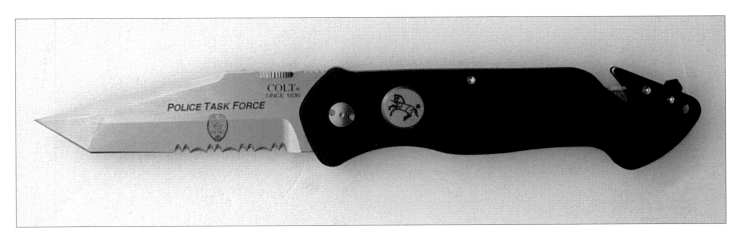

This is one of a group of Colt knives designed for emergency personnel with specialized models for firefighters, emergency medical technicians, police or rescue personnel. Designed to be readily opened or closed while wearing gloves, these are designed to be light, compact working knives for professionals. The inclusion of the glass-breaker and seat-belt cutter make them even more versatile. The auxiliary cutting blade is easily changed. Despite all of the useful features of this knife and its companion models, it is quite reasonably priced.

Closed Length: 4.8 inches
Open Length: 8 inches
Blade Length and Type: 3.3 inches, Tanto, partially serrated, single opening stud
Weight: 4.6 ounces
Grip: Aluminum with seat-belt cutter and carbide glass breaker, pocket clip
Lock: Modified liner-lock with button release

Colt Police Task Force

Source: Ontario Knife Company, P.O. Box 145, Franklinville, NY 14737, (716) 676-5527, www.ontarioknife.com

Columbia River Knife and Tool M16-13T

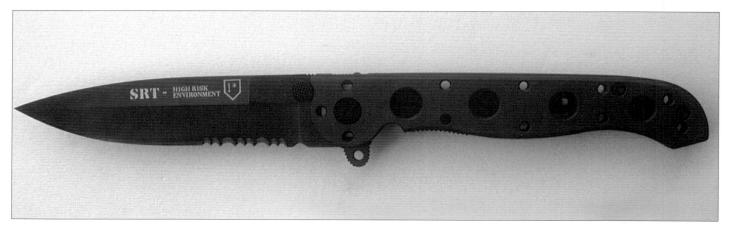

The SRT model illustrated is an excellent light law-enforcement or military folder. It combines the light weight of a titanium grip with an AUS8 stainless steel blade which has been blackened. The Lake And Walker Knife Safety (LAWKS) helps ensure the blade locks open surely, while the dual stud and Carson flipper make this a smooth and quiet opening folder.

Closed Length: 4.6 inches
Open Length: 8.2 inches
Blade Length and Type: 3.6 inches, Drop Point, partially serrated, with dual opening stud and Carson flipper
Weight: 2.9 ounces
Grip: Skeletonized aluminum with pocket clip
Lock: Liner, plus LAWKS lever safety
Source: Columbia River Knife and Tool, 9720 S. W. Hillman Ct, Suite 805, Wilsonville, OR 97070, (503) 685-50515, www.crkt.com

Columbia River Knife and Tool M16-13T

Columbia River Knife and Tool M16-14SF

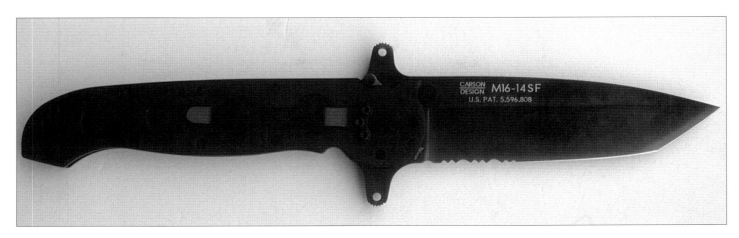

The M16-14SF combines the desirable features of the smaller M16-13T just discussed but in a larger knife. The combination of the Tanto point and crossguard make this an effective folding close-combat knife, one on which the double locking system assures the blade will remain open. It is lively in the hand and lends itself to various styles of close combat. Still, it is light enough to carry easily about the person.

Closed Length: 5.3 inches
Open Length: 9.2 inches
Blade Length and Type: 4 inches, Tanto, partially serrated, with dual opening stud and Carson flipper/ integral crossguard
Weight: 4.9 ounces
Grip: Skeletonized aluminum with pocket clip
Lock: Liner with LAWKS lever safety
Source: Columbia River Knife and Tool, 9720 S. W. Hillman Ct, Suite 805, Wilsonville, OR 97070, (503) 685-50515, www.crkt.com

Columbia River Knife and Tool M16-14SF

Columbia River Knife and Tool M16 Titanium

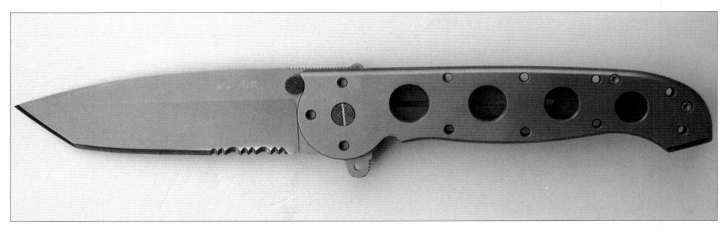

Similar to the M16-14SF but with titanium grip, this M16 is designed to stand up to hard usage even better. Like the other Columbia River folders, it is extremely quiet and smooth in opening due to the use of Teflon bearings. I emphasize that, for military or police users who might want to deploy their folding knife quietly, this is an important feature.

Closed Length: 5.3 inches
Open Length: 9.2 inches
Blade Length and Type: 4 inches, Tanto, partially serrated, with dual opening stud and Carson flipper
Weight: 5.9 ounces
Grip: Skeletonized titanium with pocket clip
Lock: Liner with LAWKS lever safety
Source: Columbia River Knife and Tool, 9720 S. W. Hillman Ct, Suite 805, Wilsonville, OR 97070, (503) 685-50515, www.crkt.com

Columbia River Knife and Tool M16 Titanium

Corsican Vendatta Knife

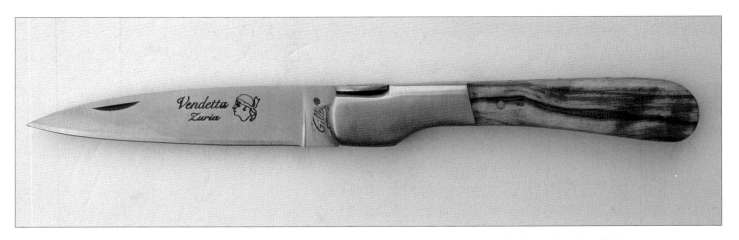

Corsica has a long tradition of blade making, though the best modern examples of this traditional Corsican knife usually come from makers in Thiers. Though this example from Fontenille retains the traditional lines of the Vendetta Knife, it uses modern stainless steel for the blade. This is a famous design that has been used for close combat in waterfront dives all over the world. The blade is well designed for thrusting or slashing, while the grip is quite comfortable and allows quick movements with the blade. The fact there is no lock for the blade, however, is certainly a detriment when compared to most modern folders. I have always liked this design and have carried one in the past, but if I have to choose between tradition and a blade less likely to close on my hand, I invariably take a folder with a blade lock.

Corsican Vendetta Knife

Closed Length: 4.6 inches
Open Length: 8.5 inches
Blade Length and Type: 3.5 inches, Drop Point
Weight: 4.4 ounces
Grip: Olive wood panels
Lock: None
Source: Fontenille-Pataud, Thiers, France, www.fontenille-pataud.com

Couteau Troupes Aeroportées Surve (French Paratroop Survival Knife)

French Paratroop Survival Knife

ring and is also supplied with a belt sheath. Since it is a fairly heavy knife, it will normally be carried on a belt or on other equipment, perhaps with paracord attached to the lanyard ring and tied to the equipment. Although many French paras and other special ops troops carry a fixed-blade fighting knife as well, the Para Survival Knife is really a pretty good utility / combat knife which can adequately serve in many roles. The fact it has remained in service for a half-century should attest to its usefulness.

Closed Length: 5.3 inches
Open Length: 9.5 inches
Blade Length and Type: 4.2 inches, Spear Point, additional utility blades
Weight: 9.4 ounces
Grip: Polymer with integral crossguards
Lock: Lever back lock
Source: S.C.C.F., France; U.S. Importer: Cutlery To Go, 2409 Pebblebrook Ct., Grand Prairie, TX 75050, (866) 975-4020, www.cutlerytogo.com

This heavy-duty folder has been the French paratroop knife since the Indochina War and has performed as a multi-task folder quite well. Its main blade can serve as a utility blade but is also capable of use in close combat. The knife also incorporates various utility blades including a saw, corkscrew, bottle opener, awl and screwdriver. The knife has a lanyard

Earnest Emerson Commander

Earnest Emerson Commander

The Commander is a medium folding combat knife, suitable for military or police usage, capable of standing up well to extended use, but still compact enough to carry well. It has been issued to U.S. and NATO special operations forces and has earned a solid reputation with the operators who have used it. Because of its popularity with military units, the Commander is available with either black or green panels. One interesting feature is the Wave or Remote Pocket Opener, a wave-shaped hook on the spine which allows the knife to be opened by hooking it on the pocket or other gear should a hand injury or other problem preclude normal use of the opening disk. Earnest Emerson knives have a reputation for good design and toughness. The Commander is no exception.

Closed Length: 5 inches
Open Length: 8.8 inches
Blade Length and Type: 3.8 inches, Drop Point, partially serrated, dual opening disk, Wave Opening feature
Weight: 5.5 ounces
Grip: G-10, with pocket clip and lanyard/wrist-loop hole
Lock: Liner
Source: Emerson Knives, Torrance, CA 90510, (310) 212-7455, www.emersonknives.com

Earnest Emerson CQC-7B

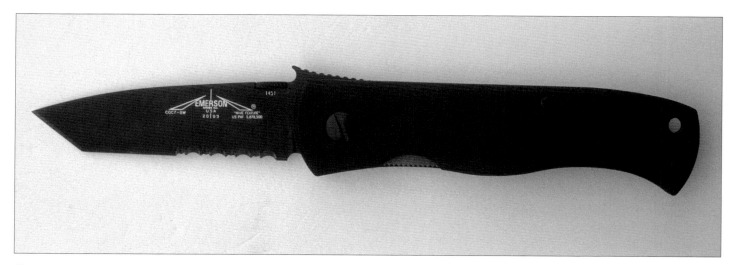

Earnest Emerson CQC-7B

The CQC has been one of the most popular folding knife designs of all time and has earned a deserved reputation for its design. I have, in fact, carried one for years and have always been very pleased with it. I would classify the CQC-7B as a light combat knife that performs like a medium one. Able to perform myriad cutting tasks or defend its

user, it rides easily in a pocket or clipped to the pocket. The CQC-7B is the type of knife that is especially well designed for the police officer, soldier or outdoorsman who wants one good folding knife which he or she can carry with confidence every day whether on or off duty.

Closed Length: 4.5 inches
Open Length: 8 inches
Blade Length and Type: 3.3 inches, Tanto, partially serrated, dual opening disk and Wave Opener
Weight: 4.3 ounces
Grip: G-10, with pocket clip and lanyard/wrist-thong hole
Lock: Liner
Source: Emerson Knives, Torrance, CA 90510, (310) 212-7455, www.emersonknives.com

Esparcia Swing Guard

This Esparcia bears some resemblance to Buck's classic 110 line of knives, at least partially because it employs a lever lock at the rear of the grip as the Buck does. It employs the wide blade popular with many Spanish users, however. The blade is stainless steel. I have always liked the Esparcia Swing Guard knives as compact folding fighting knives. When I used to work on VIP protection details in areas where I could not carry a firearm, I used to pick up folding close-combat knives locally with the idea that if I

needed to leave them behind it would be easier with a knife I had purchased locally. One style I used to look for in bazaars or flea markets was this Esparcia Swing Guard. I also used to know an ex-Spanish Foreign Legionnaire who had carried a similar knife for years. I have no doubt he had used it in close combat more than once. In simple terms I would classify this knife as one of those that often turn up for sale in bazaars or flea markets in venues where one might decide a knife for self-defense is a good idea. When I

Esparcia Swing Guard

see Esparcia knives for sale in such places, they are frequently my choice.

Closed Length: 4.5 inches
Open Length: 8 inches
Blade Length and Type: 3.3 inches, Spear Point
Weight: 6.6 ounces
Grip: Wood, with brass fittings and swing crossguard
Lock: Lever
Source: Esparcia, Spain

Extrema Ratio Fulcrum

Extrema Ratio offers five types of folder of which the Fulcrum is the most basic, yet it is still quite a heavy-duty knife. Fabricated from N690 Cobalt stainless steel coated with the Testudo anti-abrasion and anti-corrosion finish, this knife is meant to stand up to heavy use by military- or law-enforcement personnel. As with all Extrema Ratio knives, this is a sturdy service knife meant to stand up to hard usage; it is not a dainty gentleman's pocketknife. This basic model does not have a pocket clip but comes with a ballistic nylon sheath. Whether this or one of the other Extrema folders is chosen, the owner can count on a knife that will stand up to a lifetime of tough usage.

Closed Length: 5 inches
Open Length: 8.7 inches
Blade Length and Type: 3.7 inches, Tanto, partially serrated, dual opening stud
Weight: 7.1 ounces

Extrema Ratio Fulcrum

Grip: Anticorrodal aluminum with exposed steel wrist-thong slot/glass-breaker
Lock: Back lock
Source: Extrema Ratio V.le Montegrappa, 298-59100 Prato (PO), Italy. Telephone: +39 57 458 4639, www.extremaratio.com; US Source: Extrema Ratio USA, 1320 S. Glenstone #26, Springfield, MO 65804, (417) 883-9444, www.extremaratiousa.com

Extrema Ratio M.P.C.

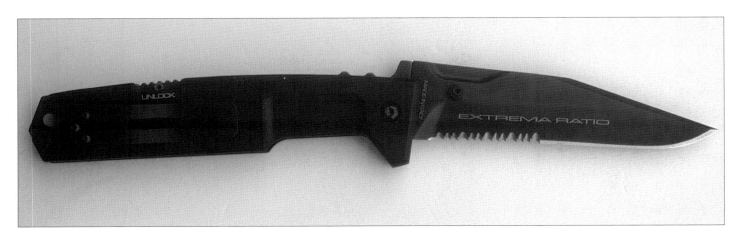

The M.P.C. is the best heavy-duty military or police folder I have examined. This is a folder that will stand up to utility or close-combat usage yet carries easily in the pocket or clipped to webbed gear. The cross bolt auxiliary lock not only augments the already strong back lock, but when applied with the knife closed virtually assures that if it should be taken away by an enemy it will not be used against its owner. This proprietary aspect has some appeal especially for law enforcement users. Other features of the M.P.C. are as discussed for the Fulcrum. I guess my final comment on the M.P.C. is that if I had to choose one folding knife for use as a military combat knife this is the one I would choose.

Closed Length: 5.8 inches
Open Length: 10.2 inches
Blade Length and Type: 4.5 inches, Clip Point, partially serrated, dual opening stud
Weight: 8.6 ounces

Extrema Ratio M.P.C.

Grip: Anticorrodal aluminum with exposed steel wrist-thong slot/glass breaker, pocket clip
Lock: Back lock with cross bolt
Source: Extrema Ratio V.le Montegrappa, 298-59100 Prato (PO), Italy. Telephone: +39 57 458 4639, www.extremaratio.com; US Source: Extrema Ratio USA, 1320 S. Glenstone #26, Springfield, MO 65804, (417) 883-9444, www.extremaratiousa.com

Gerber Applegate-Fairbairn Combat Folder

Rex Applegate wanted to offer a folder specifically designed for combat whilst retaining the characteristics of the fixed blade Applegate-Fairbairn Fighting Knife; the Combat Folder is the result. Balanced well for close combat and employing a blade that can be used effectively in slashes, cuts or thrusts, this knife is a folder that retains the feel of a fixed-blade fighting knife. Another feature that is quite useful is the crosshatched stud on the liner lock, which makes it easier to release. For the soldier, police officer, or anyone else who requires a folding knife that can be deployed as a serious fighting knife, the Applegate-Fairbairn Combat Folder is an excellent choice.

Closed Length: 5.6 inches
Open Length: 10 inches
Blade Length and Type: 4.3 inches, Spear Point, partially serrated, dual opening stud
Weight: 6.4 ounces
Grip: Grooved, glass-filled nylon, wrist-thong hole

Gerber Applegate-Fairbairn Combat Folder

Lock: Liner
Source: Gerber Legendary Blades, 14200 SW 72nd Avenue, Portland, OR 97224, (503) 639-6161, www.gerberblades.com

Gerber Applegate-Fairbairn Covert

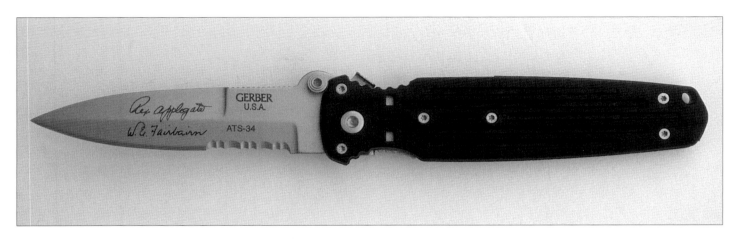

The Covert is the compact version of the A-F Combat Folder and offers an excellent option for anyone needing a compact yet effective folding fighting knife. The pocket clip allows it to be carried unobtrusively yet ready for easy access, while the Lake-Walker lock helps assure the blade will stay locked. This is an especially good choice for the soldier who carries a larger combat knife but wants an easy-to-carry fighting knife on his or her person. It will also work quite well for the police officer that carries a fighting knife as a hideout weapon. The Applegate-Fairbairn Covert has frequently been my own choice when I have wanted an easily carried folding close-combat knife.

Closed Length: 4.9 inches
Open Length: 8.5 inches
Blade Length and Type: 3.5 inches, Spear Point, partially serrated, dual opening stud
Weight: 4.0 ounces

Gerber Applegate-Fairbairn Covert

Grip: Grooved, glass-filled nylon, pocket clip, wrist-thong hole
Lock: Liner and Lake-Walker manual lever safety
Source: Gerber Legendary Blades, 14200 SW 72nd Avenue, Portland, OR 97224, (503) 639-6161, www.gerberblades.com

Gerber Spectre

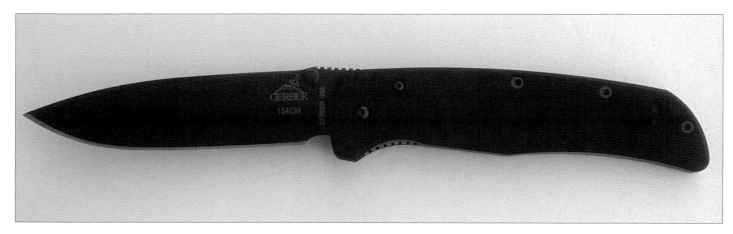

The Spectre is a light, compact stainless steel folder well suited for general usage. Gerber offers an assortment of well made light utility folders of which the Spectre is one of the best for military or police usage. The Spectre can also serve as an everyday folding knife, one that is of such high quality that it will last a lifetime.

Closed Length: 4.3 inches
Open Length: 8 inches
Blade Length and Type: 3.3 inches; Drop Point, dual opening stud;
Weight: 3.6 ounces
Grip: Checkered G-10, with pocket clip and wrist-thong- or lanyard hole
Lock: Liner
Source: Gerber Legendary Blades, 14200 SW 72nd Avenue, Portland, OR 97224, (503) 639-6161, www.gerberblades.com

Gerber Spectre

Katz Knives Kagemusha

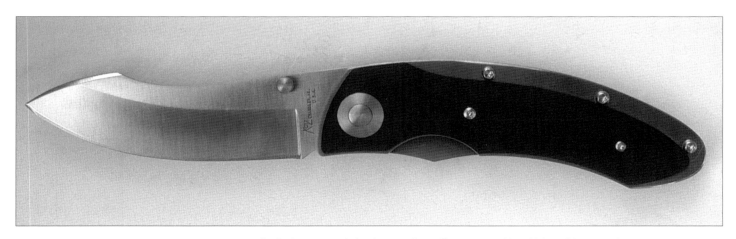

According to Katz Knives, Kagemusha means "Secret Ninja". The blade, which Katz designates as a "Ninja-Point", is basically a Drop Point with an upswept spine. The result is a rather elegant knife that is sturdier than most light folders. I think I would designate it as a medium folder in toughness. The steel frame of the grip offers a striking point and might work as a window breaker. It is a bit blunt so I would have to try it to be sure. I am rather a fan of Katz Knives, which I find show good design and quality while retaining a reasonable price. Though not a pure folding fighter such as the Applegate-Fairbairn, I would nevertheless be content to carry the Kagemusha for that mission.

Closed Length: 4.6 inches
Open Length: 8 inches
Blade Length and Type: 3.5 inches, "Ninja-Point", single opening stud
Grip: Checkered Kraton, with stainless steel border, pocket clip

Katz Knives Kagemusha

Lock: Liner
Source: Katz Knives, P.O. Box 730, Chandler, AZ 85224, (480) 786-9334, www.katzkn@aol.com

Kershaw BOA

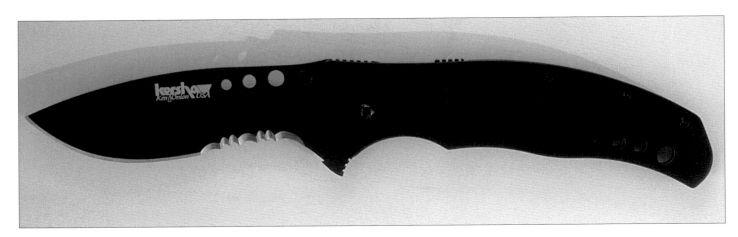

This Ken Onion design is a high-quality light duty / combat knife capable of utility or close-combat usage. The assisted opening system makes this knife almost as easy to operate as an automatic yet without the legal restrictions that automatic knives can face in some areas. Another clever feature is the hooked stud, which acts as a lower crossguard when the blade is open, but which protrudes through the frame when the knife is closed. By hitting this with the index finger, the spring-loaded blade will deploy. It may also be deployed by slight pressure on the opening stud. As with automatic knives, it is important that assisted opening knives have a secondary safety to prevent the knife opening while in the pocket. The secondary sliding safety on the BOA is located just behind the index-finger opening stud and may be slid off just before the finger hits this protrusion to open the knife. This is a very well designed quickly deployable knife, another good choice for a light-duty combat knife.

Kershaw BOA

Closed Length: 4.8 inches
Open Length: 8 inches
Blade Length and Type: 3.5 inches, Drop Point, partially serrated, single opening stud and index-finger stud
Grip: 60661-T6 aircraft aluminum, with pocket clip and lanyard/wrist-thong hole
Lock: Liner, second sliding safety lock
Source: Kershaw Knives, 25300 SW Parkway Ave., Wilsonville, OR 97070, (503) 682-1966, www.kershawknives.com

Al Mar SERE 2000

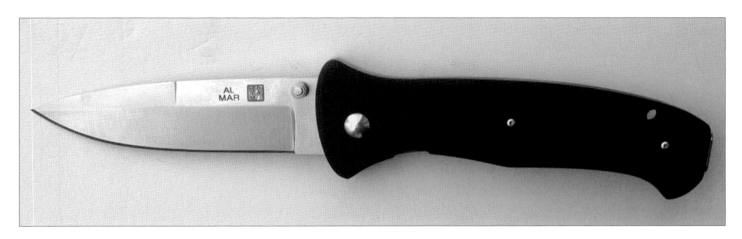

The SERE 2000 is the descendant of Al Mar's famous SERE Attack knives which were initially designed for the U.S. Army Special Forces escape and evasion course. SERE stands for the four basic tenets of that course – Survival, Escape, Resistance, Evasion. The original SERE was a big, heavy-duty folder usable as a general combat knife, a survival knife, or a fighting knife. The SERE 2000 is a little over an inch smaller in closed length and is lighter, but it is still quite an effective medium-duty military or law enforcement knife. Al Mar's knives have used quality Japanese steels as long as I have been using them, and my original SERE certainly held up to rough usage in various parts of the world. I normally carried it in a belt pouch or in a cargo or jacket pocket, however. The SERE 2000, on the other hand, carries readily in a trouser pocket and offers a lot of knife for its size.

Al Mar SERE 2000

Closed Length: 4.8 inches
Open Length: 8.4 inches
Blade Length and Type: 3.5 inches, Drop Point, dual opening stud
Weight: 6 ounces
Grip: Textured G-10, pocket clip and lanyard/wrist-thong hole
Lock: Liner
Source: Al Mar Knives, P.O. Box 2295, Tualatin, OR 97062, (503) 670-9080, www.almarknives.com

Master of Defense CQD (Close Quarters Defense)

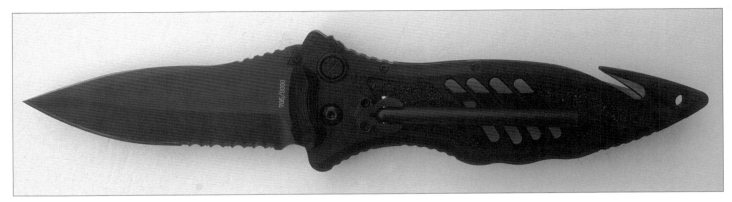

Designed specifically as a special ops folder, the CQD owes much of its design to well-known close-combat trainer Duane Dieter. Among its desirable features is the plunge-lock system which locks up the knife very securely yet allows the blade to be released without having to place the fingers in its path. The secondary sliding lock is another desirable feature. In a military- or police-duty knife, the window breaker and secondary ATAC (Advanced Tactical) support blade are both very useful. The support blade allows seat belts to be cut safely or lines to be cut without opening the

blade. The support blade may easily be changed as well. Another useful feature is the rigging spike, which easily folds out from the knife's body. The CQD comes with a pocket clip and also with one of two sheaths – one ballistic nylon and one Kydex. The ballistic nylon sheath is designed so that it may be attached easily to the sheath of the MOD ATAC. The CQD is an impressive knife, well conceived to serve the special ops community for which it is intended but also viable for law enforcement or others who need a versatile combat knife.

MOD CQD

Closed Length: 5.8 inches
Open Length: 9.5 inches
Blade Length and Type: 3.5 inches Spear Point, partially serrated, dual opening stud
Weight: 8.2 ounces
Grip: Milled aluminum, black anodized, with window breaker and shielded support blade, with folding spike
Lock: Plunge lock with secondary sliding safety lock
Source: Masters of Defense, 256-A Industrial Park Dr. Waynesville, NC 28786, (828) 452-4158, www.mastersofdefense.com

Mercworx Atropos

Although there are other good heavy-duty folders, the Atropos ranks with the MOD CQD and the Extrema Ratio M.P.C. as my own top choices for serious military or police usage. As already stated in the section on fixed-blade knives, I like the Mercworx blade style; it is both elegant and efficient, in my opinion a combination that is tough to beat. The Atropos uses a BG-42 blade combined with a titanium body for a combination of strength and durability. The .060 liner lock is thick enough to stand up to heavy usage, as is the hardened steel pin that holds the blade in place. Another desirable aspect of the Atropos is that it is the largest in a series of "Three Fates" knives from Mercworx. Each is proportional to the Atropos, with the Lachesis the medium-sized option and the Clotho the smallest of the three. Anyone who likes the Mercworx design and style can therefore purchase a brace of knives to fit various needs. The Atropos can serve as the heavy-duty service knife while a Clotho could ride in the pocket on a daily basis. I have, in fact, started carrying a Clotho as a compact folding fighting knife.

Mercworx Atropos

Closed Length: 5.5 inches
Open Length: 9.4 inches
Blade Length and Type: 4 inches, Drop Point, single opening stud
Weight: 7.0 ounces
Grip: Linen Micarta with wrist-thong hole
Lock: Liner
Source: Mercworx, 235 Main St., #287, Madison, NJ 07940, (908) 619-1013, www.mercworx.com

SOG Flash

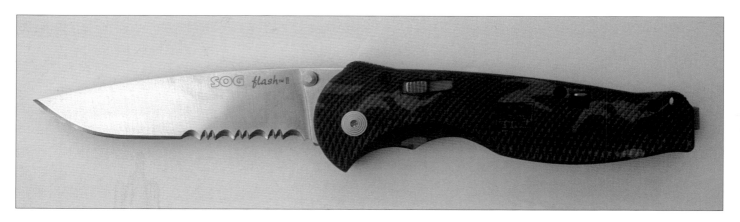

This is another light-duty or combat knife that makes use of assisted opening technology, in this case the SAT (SOG Assisted Technology) system. One aspect of this knife that I like a lot is the piston locking system which allows the blade to be released by pulling down on the piston lock with the fingers out of the path of the closing blade. The secondary lock is located on the grip in a position that requires some effort to release. This is good in that it makes it less likely that the blade will be opened inadvertently in the pocket, but it does slow opening somewhat. In addition to the camouflage handle, the Flash is also available with a black handle. The assisted opening system is quite useful, but one must practice with the Flash to get used to the secondary safety lock. Still, I rate this a good compact combat knife.

SOG Flash

Closed Length: 4.5 inches
Open Length: 8 inches
Blade Length and Type: 3.5 inches, Drop Point, partially serrated, dual opening stud
Weight: 3 ounces
Grip: Camouflage Zytel, pocket clip, lanyard/wrist-thong hole
Lock: Piston, with secondary sliding safety lock
Source: SOG, 6521 212th St, SW, Lynnwood, WA 98036, (425) 771-6230, www.sogknives.com

Spyderco Assist

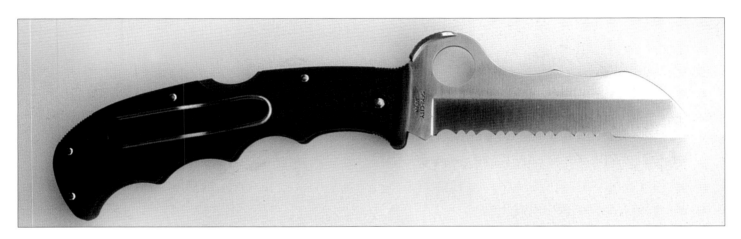

Although originally designed for fire and rescue personnel, the Assist makes a good survival knife for fishermen, boaters or others who might need a knife to "assist" them in an emergency. The survival whistle may never be used, but it is certainly a useful adjunct if one becomes lost or injured. The serrated blade is especially well designed for cutting rope by placing the rope between the grip and the serrations on the blade, then using the finger grooves on the blade's spine to press against the rope. A version of the Assist with a retractable carbide tip glass breaker is also available. The Cobra Hood feature above the thumb-opening hole is also a useful idea as it aids in opening when the hands are cold or wearing gloves but also offers a thumb position when the blade is open.

Closed Length: 5 inches
Open Length: 8.3 inches;
Blade Length and Type: 3.5 inches, modified Sheep's Foot, partially serrated, thumb opening hole with "Cobra Hood"

Spyderco Assist

Weight: 3.9 ounces
Grip: FRN (Fiberglass Reinforced Nylon), with a built-in survival whistle, pocket clip and lanyard/wrist-thong hole
Lock: Lever; Source: Spyderco, Inc., 820 Spyderco Way, Golden, CO 80403, (303) 279-8383, www.spyderco.com

Spyderco Bob Lum

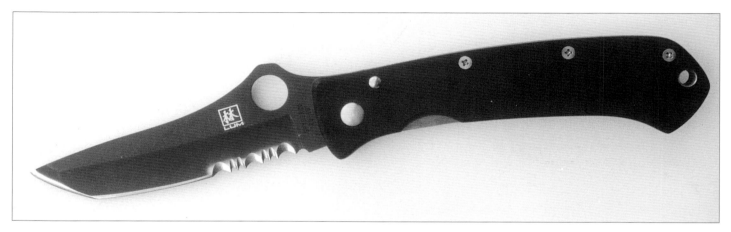

This is the Spyderco for those who like the Tanto Point. Its blackened blade and black G-10 scales help make it a good choice as a military- or law enforcement light-duty combat knife. The thumb opening system and the Tanto blade are good features should this knife be used as a fighting knife, though its most likely application is as a utility / combat knife which can serve for close combat if necessary.

Closed Length: 5 inches
Open Length: 8.7 inches
Blade Length and Type: 3.5 inches, Tanto, partially serrated, with thumb opening hole
Weight: 5.1 ounces
Grip: G-10, with pocket clip and lanyard/wrist-thong hole
Lock: Liner
Source: Spyderco, Inc., 820 Spyderco Way, Golden, CO 80403, (303) 279-8383, www.spyderco.com

Spyderco Bob Lum

Spyderco Matriarch

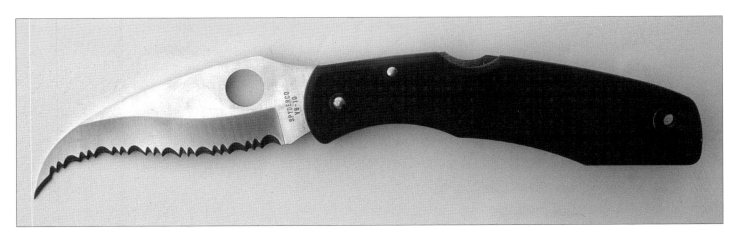

The Matriarch evolved from the heavier civilian model as a wicked slashing weapon for undercover law enforcement personnel. Even with minimal close-combat training, its sharp claw-like blade can inflict serious wounds with each slash. Unlike most knives originally designed as law enforcement blades, this one has little general utility application. It is a light yet wicked weapon designed to inflict serious wounds on an attacking criminal.

Closed Length: 4.8 inches
Open Length: 8.2 inches
Blade Length and Type: 3.2 inches, fully serrated "claw", with thumb opening hole
Weight: 2.8 ounces
Grip: FRN, pocket clip and lanyard/wrist-thong hole
Lock: Lever
Source: Spyderco, Inc., 820 Spyderco Way, Golden, CO 80403, (303) 279-8383, www.spyderco.com

Spyderco Matriarch

Spyderco Native III

Spyderco has continued to improve the Native to make it a very ergonomic little knife. Though very compact, its grip is well designed to allow a sure hold, which will not slip forward. This is a light-duty or combat knife but is smaller than most others in this category. As a result, those who work in suits or other clothing, which might not allow the carry of a large knife, can still have an effective close-combat weapon in the Native.

Closed Length: 3.9 inches
Open Length: 7 inches
Blade Length and Type: 2.5 inches, Drop Point, opening hole
Weight: 2.4 ounces
Grip: Textured FRN, pocket clip, lanyard/wrist-thong hole
Lock: Rocker back
Source: Spyderco, Inc., 820 Spyderco Way, Golden, CO 80403, (303) 279-8383, www.spyderco.com

Spyderco Native III

Spyderco Police Model

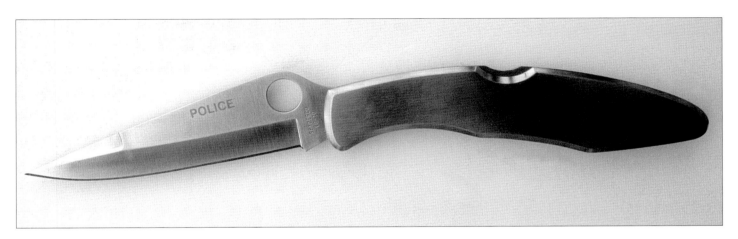

First introduced in 1984, the Police Model helped set the standard for law enforcement folding knives. I have used one myself for many years and have found it utterly reliable and durable. The David Boye dish in the lever-lock release is a useful feature, as it greatly lowers any chance of inadvertently releasing the blade while taking a tight grip on the knife. The Police Model's blade design allows it to serve as a close-combat knife if necessary, though it will be used far more often as a general-purpose folder. Although the model shown has a plain blade, serrations are available if desired for cutting seat belts, rope, etc. Many agencies like the smooth stainless handle as it allows this knife to be easily serial-numbered, have the badge or logo engraved, or otherwise marked. This is one of the best choices available for a medium-duty police folding knife.

Spyderco Police Model

Closed Length: 5.4 inches
Open Length: 9.4 inches
Blade Length and Type: 4.1 inches, Clip Point, thumb hole
Weight: 5.5 ounces
Grip: Stainless steel
Lock: Lever
Source: Spyderco, Inc., 820 Spyderco Way, Golden, CO 80403, (303) 279-8383, www.spyderco.com

Swiss Soldier's Knife

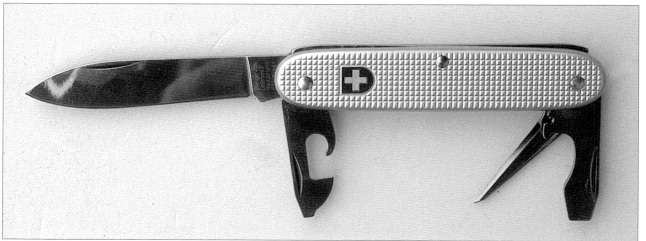

Swiss Soldier's Knife

The "Swiss Army Knife" has become so ubiquitous around the world that it is easy to forget that it truly originated as an issue item for the Swiss Army. The knife illustrated is the current issue knife for enlisted soldiers in the Swiss Army. While some Swiss Army knives incorporate two dozen or more tools, this compact issued knife only includes a primary cutting blade, an awl, a large screwdriver combined with a bottle opener, and a small screwdriver combined with a can opener. Traditionally, the officer's issue knife also incorporates a corkscrew. There are two Swiss manufacturers of the Swiss Army Knife – Victorinox and Wenger – each of which produces 50% of the knives for the Swiss Army. Throughout the rest of the world, they compete for business. I have owned four or five Swiss Army knives over the years, some with numerous blades and tools. All have served well and proven themselves invaluable companion knives.

Closed Length: 3.6 inches
Open Length: 6.4 inches
Blade Length and Type: 2.5 inches, Drop Point, additional utility blades
Weight: 2.4 ounces
Grip: Checkered aluminum
Lock: None
Source: Victorinox or Wenger, Switzerland.

Timberline Worden Tactical

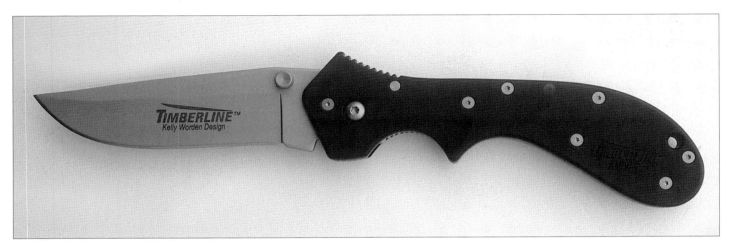

This Kelly Worden design is intended to provide a reasonably priced heavy-duty combat knife, which still has many desirable features. The grip, for example, is ergonomically designed with finger grooves that position the hand well and surely for exerting downward pressure on the blade. The use of Teflon washers is another plus, as it allows the knife to open smoothly and quietly. The thumb ramp, which is dished out of the Zytel, is an aid to hitting the opening stud quickly and should be especially helpful if the hands and/or knife are damp. The bead-blasted stainless steel blade combines durability with less reflectiveness. There is also a medium-sized version of this tactical knife as well.

Timberline Worden Tactical

Closed Length: 5.7 inches
Open Length: 9.5 inches
Blade Length and Type: 3.9 inches, Clip Point, dual opening stud
Weight: 7 ounces
Grip: Zytel, pocket clip and lanyard/wrist-thong hole
Lock: Liner
Source: Timberline Knives, P.O. Box 600, Getzville, NY 14068-0600, (716) 877-2200, www.timberlineknives.com

TOPS Ghost Rider

TOPS Ghost Rider

As with TOPS' fixed-blade knives, the emphasis with the Ghost Rider is on sturdiness and functionality. I like the pebbled grip with the thumb-cut to allow ease of opening. I also like the flat gray blade finish. In addition to the Tanto Point, the Ghost Rider is also available with Clip Point ("Hunter's Point" in TOPS terminology) and Spear Point. Designed as a tactical knife for police or military usage, the Night Rider should serve well.

Closed Length: 5.4 inches
Open Length: 9.8 inches
Blade Length and Type: 4.3 inches, Tanto, single opening stud
Weight: 6.8 ounces
Grip: Pebbled G10, pocket clip
Lock: Liner
Source: TOPS Knives, P.O. Box 2544, Idaho Falls, ID 83403, (208) 542-0113, www.topsknives.com

Benchmade AFO

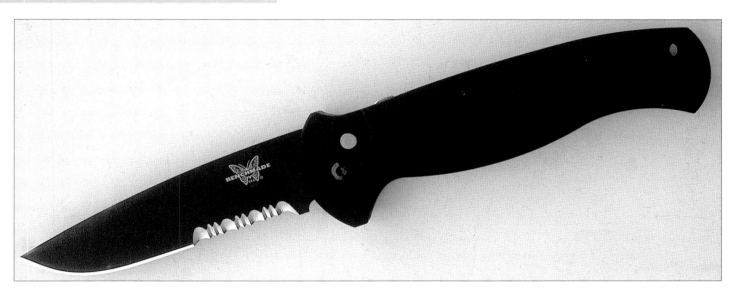

Benchmade has "carved out" a major niche in the military and law enforcement markets for its high quality automatic knives. The AFO is widely used among the U.S. armed forces and has a military procurement number (NSN-1095-01-446-4348) and the military designation "Knife, Combat (Auto)". The stainless steel blade is available in matte finish or blackened. The AFO is designed for tough usage and would qualify as a medium-duty automatic well suited for military or police usage. Its easily operated safety lock assures that the knife will stay closed or open once it is applied.

Closed Length: 4.7 inches
Open Length: 8.4 inches
Blade Length and Type: 3.6 inches, Drop Point, partially serrated

Benchmade AFO

Grip: T-6 aluminum, pocket clip, lanyard/wrist-thong hole
Opening System: Press-button;
Lock: Sliding integrated safety
Source: Benchmade Knife Company, 300 Beavercreek Rd., Oregon City, OR 97046, (503) 655-6223, www.benchmade.com

Benchmade Auto Stryker

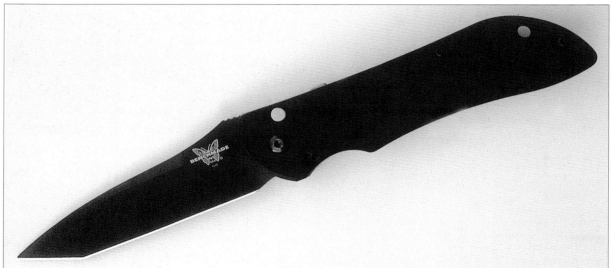

Benchmade Auto Stryker

The Auto Stryker is another Benchmade auto with a military procurement number (NSN-1095-01-456-4457). The stainless Drop Point Tanto blade is well designed for puncturing or thrusting in close combat. The combination of blackened blade and anodized aluminum grip offer a non-reflective combo for military or tactical law enforcement usage. As with all of the Benchmade autos, this is a well designed knife with an effective secondary safety to give the user confidence while it is riding in the pocket.

Closed Length: 4.7 inches
Open Length: 8.3 inches
Blade Length and Type: 3.7 inches, Tanto

Weight: 4.1 inches
Grip: T-6 aluminum, belt clip, lanyard/wrist-thong hole
Opening System: Press-button
Lock: Sliding safety
Source: Benchmade Knife Company, 300 Beavercreek Rd., Oregon City, OR 97046, (503) 655-6223, www.benchmade.com

Benchmade Mini-Auto Stryker

The Mini-Auto Stryker has the same basic features as the full-sized version, though the example illustrated has the bright blade. The greatest appeal of this automatic is that it is compact enough that plain clothes police officers can easily carry it in a pocket, yet it is still an effective knife. It would also make a good choice for military personnel who carry a larger fixed blade knife and want an easily deployed automatic knife to carry about the person.

Closed Length: 4.2 inches
Open Length: 7.1 inches
Blade Length and Type: 2.9 inches, Tanto, partially serrated
Weight: 2.9 ounces
Grip: T-6 aluminum, pocket clip, lanyard/wrist-thong hole
Opening System: Ambidextrous axis thumb button
Lock: Sliding safety
Source: Benchmade Knife Company, 300 Beavercreek Rd., Oregon City, OR 97046, (503) 655-6223, www.benchmade.com

Benchmade Mini-Auto Stryker

Benchmade Pardue Axis Auto

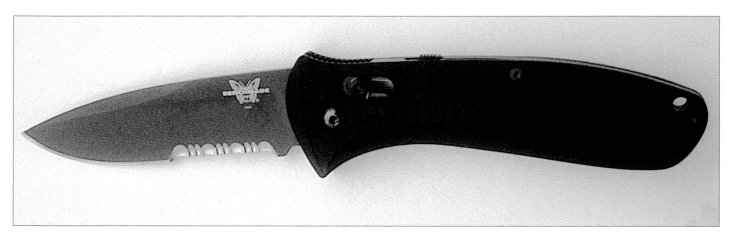

Benchmade Pardue Axis Auto

The Axis lock is a very positive locking system, which uses a steel bar that spans the space between the liners and engages a ramped notch in the blade's tang. Two omega-style springs provide the inertia for the locking bar to engage the tang. The combination of the Axis system with automatic opening make this an outstanding knife. To open the knife, all that is necessary is to draw the Axis button backward against spring tension. The blade is released the same way. The addition of the sliding safety lock makes this knife virtually foolproof against opening inadvertently, an inherent problem with some automatic knives. In combination with the blackened stainless steel blade and anodized aluminum grip, this creates a superb military or police automatic knife.

Closed Length: 4.9 inches
Open Length: 8.2 inches
Blade Length and Type: 3.4 inches, Drop Point, partially serrated
Weight: 5.6 ounces
Grip: T-6 aluminum, pocket clip, lanyard/wrist-thong hole
Opening System: Ambidextrous axis thumb button
Lock: Sliding safety
Source: Benchmade Knife Company, 300 Beavercreek Rd., Oregon City, OR 97046, (503) 655-6223, www.benchmade.com

Gerber Emerson Alliance

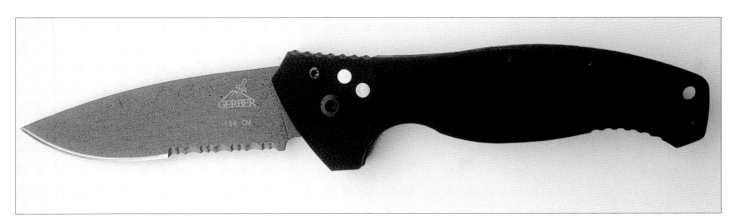

The Alliance is a high-quality, medium-duty police or law enforcement automatic. Large enough to be used for close combat or light general utility purposes, it is still compact enough or light enough to carry easily about the person. One of its best points is the cross bolt safety lock which may be easily pushed off by the thumb just prior to initiating the automatic action by pressing the release button. Its spring mechanism is strong and sure and opens quickly, then is easily locked open with the cross bolt. An interesting aspect of the opening system about which one should be aware is that the Alliance may be opened in either of two ways: the cross bolt safety may be released, then the operating button pressed; or the operating button may be pressed, at which point it will stay depressed, then the cross bolt may be operated, which opens the knife. In either case, two operations are necessary to open the blade. I like this auto quite a lot and expect to see it in service with a substantial number of military or police users.

Gerber Emerson Alliance

Closed Length: 5.3 inches
Open Length: 8.8 inches
Blade Length and Type: 3.5 inches, Drop Point, partially serrated
Weight: 5.0 ounces
Grip: Anodized aluminum, pocket clip, lanyard/wrist-thong hole
Opening System: Press-button
Lock: Cross bolt
Source: Gerber Legendary Blades, 14200 SW 72nd Avenue, Portland, OR 97224, (503) 639-6161, www.gerberblades.com

Hubertus

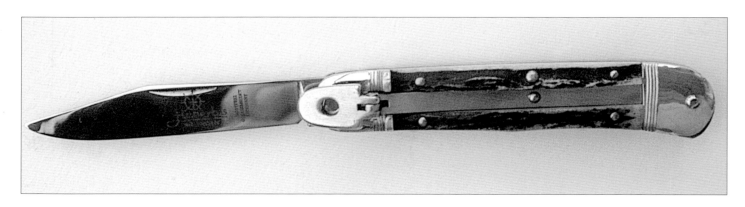

The German firm of Hubertus has produced high-quality automatic knives for decades and continues to offer them in many varieties today. Three basic sizes – 8 cm, 10 cm and 11 cm – of Hubertus knives are generally available. The example illustrated is a 10-cm knife. Various types of grip panels are also offered, though the stag illustrated is most often associated with Hubertus auto knives. Other panels available include Micarta and ebony. There is also a swing guard model designed for close combat. Although the Hubertus does not have a secondary safety lock, the lever lock system is normally quite secure if the lock is folded against the frame when the blade is in the open or closed position. I have been a great fan of Hubertus knives for many years. Though they are primarily designed as utility automatic knives, they have certainly been used as combat knives by both military and police officers.

Hubertus

Closed Length: 4 inches
Open Length: 7 inches
Blade Length and Type: 3 inches, Clip Point
Weight: 4 ounces
Grip: Stag with brass fittings
Opening System: Folding lever
Lock: Lever lock
Source: Hubertus, Solingen, Germany

Ladya

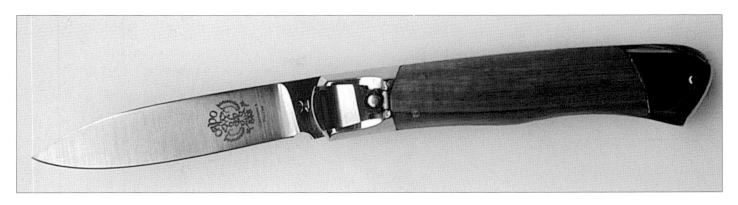

The Ladya, which translates as "Lady", is about as feminine as an Amazon or a Russian female shot-putter. This is one of the few really sturdy automatic knives that can stand up to combat usage. Designed with a heavy spring and a lever lock, the Ladya is a serious knife – serious enough that it is issued to Russian *Spetsnaz* and other special operations troops. Anyone with prejudices against Russian products based on the assumption that they are poor in quality is in for a surprise with the Ladya. This is a tightly fitted, high-quality knife, one of my favorites among autos. I should note, however,

that the Ladya is not for those with weak hands. The spring is strong enough that it takes a bit of effort to close the blade. The comments I have already made about the lever locking system apply to the Ladya as well.

Closed Length: 4.6 inches
Open Length: 7.9 inches
Blade Length and Type: 3 inches, Drop Point
Weight: 5 ounces
Grip: Wood panels, steel fittings
Opening System: Lever
Lock: Lever lock
Source: Russia

Ladya

Masters of Defense CQD (Close Quarters Defense) Auto

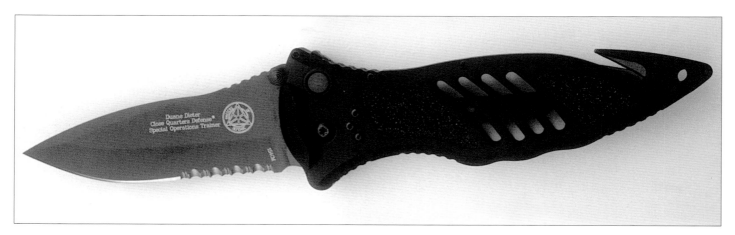

The CQD Auto has the same features as the standard folding version but with the addition of an automatic opening capability. The same button that acts as the blade release on the standard CQD functions as the operating button for the automatic version. The sliding lock on the extended hilt secures the blade in position when closed or open. Unlike many automatic knives, the CQD is designed as a true heavy-duty service knife capable of long-term combat usage and designed to function effectively for close combat if needed. The multi-use hilt with the support blade and window breaker among other features makes this knife well suited to military special operations issue. Since this really is not a pocket automatic knife it does not include a pocket clip. Instead, it comes in a sheath designed for attachment to military or police webbed gear.

Closed Length: 5.8 inches
Open Length: 9.5 inches
Blade Length and Type: 3.5 inches, Spear Point, partially serrated, dual opening stud

MOD CQD Auto

Weight: 8.2 ounces
Grip: Milled aluminum, black anodized, with window breaker and shielded support blade
Opening System: Press-button
Lock: Sliding safety
Source: Masters of Defense, 256-A Industrial Park Dr. Waynesville, NC 28786, (828) 452-4158, www.mastersofdefense.com

Microtech QD Scarab

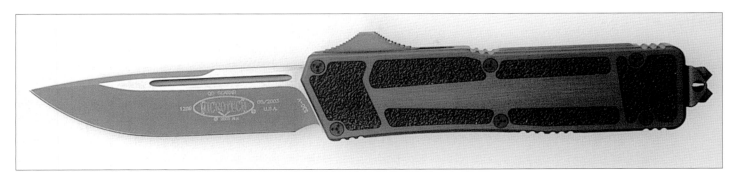

Microtech QD Scarab

The QD Scarab is an extremely high-quality "out-the-front" automatic knife. The advantage of the spring-loaded blade deploying from the front rather than swinging open is most apparent when operating in close quarters. Although the QD Scarab does not incorporate an auxiliary locking system, the fact that the spring must "load" during the initial process of pushing the sliding button to deploy or close the knife makes it extremely safe in either the closed or open position. It is therefore unlikely that inadvertent pressure will open or close the knife. This system allows the knife to be stored or carried for long periods without worrying that the spring will lose temper, since the blade is not under spring tension. The QD Scarab is designed as a knife for military or police special operators and comes with a sheath that contains a small diamond sharpener for touching up the blade in the field. The QD Scarab is very slim and quite easy to carry about the person. Its high quality combined with the "out-the-front" opening capability make it very popular with military special ops personnel who carry it as a utility automatic knife, which can be used to cut parachute shrouds or perform other duties. Since the blade can be deployed while the hand has a firm hold on the knife, it also makes a good last-ditch close-combat knife when an opponent is grappling with the operator.

Closed Length: 4.6 inches
Open Length: 8 inches
Blade Length and Type: 3.5 inches, Clip Point
Weight: 5 ounces
Grip: T6 aluminum, anodized with anti-slip inserts, pocket clip, lanyard/wrist-thong hole, glass breaker
Opening System: Top-release button
Lock: None
Source: Micro Technology, 932 36th Ct., SW Vero Beach, FL 32968, (772) 569-3058, www.microtechknives.com

Microtech UMS (Uniformed Military Services)

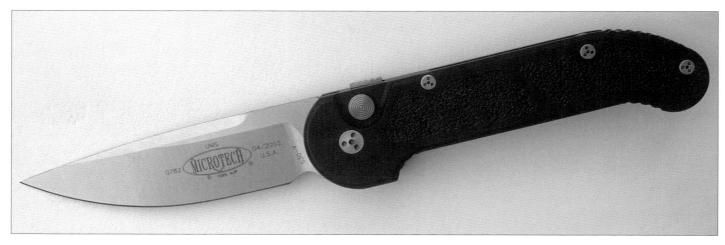

As with the previous Microtech Automatic discussed, the UMS shows extremely high quality and reflects the fact that a substantial portion of the company's production goes to military and law enforcement users who expect a long-lasting, functional knife. The UMS is a conventional side-opening automatic, which is very sure in operation. The easily operated sliding safety atop the grip helps assure that the UMS's blade stays closed while in the pocket or the scabbard, or that it stays open once it is deployed. As with all Microtech autos that I have examined, the grip on the UMS is very well designed to be non-slip and comfortable. This is another Microtech automatic knife that is well proven in military and police service.

Closed Length: 4.6 inches
Open Length: 8 inches
Blade Length and Type: 3.4 inches, Clip Point

Microtech UMS

Weight: 5 ounces
Grip: T6 aluminum with anti-slip inserts, pocket clip
Opening System: Press-button
Lock: Sliding safety
Source: Micro Technology, 932 36th Ct., SW Vero Beach, FL 32968, (772) 569-3058, www.microtechknives.com

Mikov

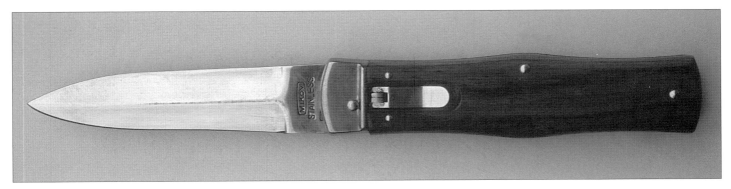

The Mikov is excellent value. One of the few automatic knives designed for military close-combat usage, those who could acquire one have prized the Mikov for years. Its Spear Point blade, strong spring action, and lever locking system allow the Mikov to perform heavier duty than most other automatics. The lever locking system is especially good since the lever folds flat into the grip when not needed, making it even less likely that it will be operated inadvertently. I have used Mikovs for years and have been very pleased with them. This knife has also been popular with special operations troops from many countries when they have managed to acquire it. Although the example illustrated has wooden scales, the Mikov is also available with ABS and stag scales. For sporting or utility use, examples are also available with conventionally opening auxiliary saw blades, corkscrews or bottle openers. More than once I have chosen the Mikov as a concealment close-combat knife when working on security jobs in developing countries.

Mikov

Closed Length: 4.7 inches
Open Length: 8.5 inches
Blade Length and Type: 3.5 inches, Spear Point
Weight: 5.0 ounces
Grip: Jacaranda wood
Opening System: Lever
Lock: Lever lock
Source: www.mikovknives.com

Pro-Tech Godfather

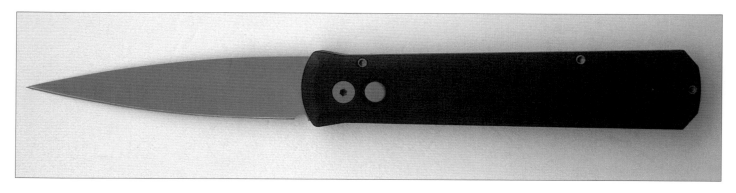

The Godfather is designed as an automatic close-combat weapon, hence the Spear Point. Pro-Tech knives are of good quality and open with authority. I prefer that automatic knives have some type of secondary safety lock, which the Pro-Tech knives do not, but they do use an activation button which is set flush with the grip which helps prevent accidental opening or closing to some extent. Pro-Tech offers a good basic automatic knife at a reasonable price. The black grip and bead-blasted grip of the Godfather enhance its tactical use. A substantial number of U.S. law enforcement personnel use Pro-Techs and are happy with them.

Closed Length: 5.3 inches
Open Length: 9.5 inches
Blade Length and Type: 4 inches,
   Spear Point
Weight: 4 ounces
Grip: Black T-6 aluminum, with belt clip
Opening System: Press-button
Lock: None
Source: Pro-Tech Knives, 11009
   Shoemaker Ave., Santa Fe Springs,
   CA 90670, (562) 903-0678,
   www.protechknives.com

Pro-Tech Godfather

Pro-Tech Tactical Response III

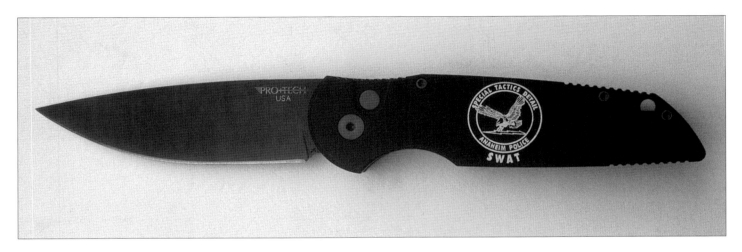

While the Godfather series are designed as close-combat autos, the Tactical Response is a more general use automatic knife for police or military personnel. The titanium nitrite-coated blade is non-reflective, as is the grip. The knife is compact enough to carry easily on an assault vest or clipped to a pocket. This is a well made tactical automatic knife, though since it lacks a secondary lock it must be handled with care, especially when closed.

Closed Length: 4.5 inches
Open Length: 8 inches
Blade Length and Type: 3.5 inches, Drop Point
Weight: 3.6 ounces
Grip: Anodized T-6 aircraft aluminum, pocket clip, lanyard/wrist-thong hole
Opening System: Press-button
Lock: None
Source: Pro-Tech Knives, 11009 Shoemaker Ave., Santa Fe Springs, CA 90670, (562) 903-0678, www.protechknives.com

Pro-Tech Tactical Response III

MULTI-TOOLS

Gerber Multi-Plier

Gerber Multi-Plier

does the multi-tool incorporate many of the same features as the Swiss Army Knife, but it also includes pliers and wire cutters strong enough to perform most tasks. Specialized multi-tools are offered for demolition personnel as well. The inclusion of the knife blades on most contemporary multi-tools allows them to substitute for the folding knife if one chooses to carry just this implement. Many military personnel, however, carry a fixed-blade combat knife and a multi-tool or a folding fighting/combat knife along with the multi-tool. As its title implies, this is a tool rather than a knife, but inclusion of a multi-tool in one's equipment allows the choice of a fighting knife rather than a more utilitarian combat knife for certain missions. While other multi-tools employ a system whereby the pliers fold out of the blade, the Gerber uses a telescoping system.

Closed Length: 5 inches
Open Length: 6.6 inches
Weight: 7.8 ounces
Tools Included: Pliers, wire cutters, crimper, Drop-Point knife, Sheepsfoot serrated knife, Phillips screwdriver, large-, medium- and small flathead screwdrivers, lanyard ring, can opener, bottle opener, file, ruler
Source: Gerber Legendary Blades, 14200 SW 72nd Avenue, Portland, OR 97224, (503) 639-6161, www.gerberblades.com

The multi-tool has become a staple with law enforcement and military personnel as well as with outdoorsmen and craftsmen. Not only

Leatherman Squirt

Leatherman Squirt

so small that it may be carried easily in addition to various other knives or tools. It is also especially well suited to carry in a compact survival kit of the type the Special Air Service or other units carry on the belt in case they must escape and evade. In addition to being functional, the Squirt is designed to be attractive as well since it is offered in blue, red or gray. This is an outstanding little multi-tool, one especially well suited for plain clothes law enforcement officers as well as anyone else who might need a tool yet does not want to carry a large knife or multi-tool around with them.

Closed Length: 2.2 inches
Open Length: 3.8 inches
Weight: 1.8 ounces
Tools Included: Needlenose pliers, straight knife, wire cutters, extra-small screwdriver, medium screwdriver, flat Phillips screwdriver, file, bottle opener, awl, key ring attachment
Source: Leatherman, P. O. Box 20595, Portland, OR 97294, (503) 253-7826, www.leatherman.com

Though the Squirt is very tiny, its pliers and wire cutters will handle surprisingly tough jobs. The Squirt is

Leatherman Wave

Leatherman Wave

accessed when the Wave is closed, thus adding great versatility. Falling between the Squirt and the Wave are an assortment of other Leatherman Tools capable of performing a wide variety of tasks. There is even a model – the Crunch – with locking pliers. The Leatherman tool, of whatever size, has a reputation for quality and, along with the other excellent multi-tools from Gerber and SOG, has become a virtual necessity among combat troops and law enforcement, fire and rescue personnel.

Closed Length: 4 inches
Open Length: 6.2 inches
Weight: 7.6 ounces
Tools Included: Needlenose pliers, regular pliers, wire cutters, hard wire cutters, Clip-Point knife, serrated knife, diamond-coated file, wood/metal file, saw, scissors, extra-small screwdriver, small screwdriver, medium screwdriver, large screwdriver, Phillips screwdriver, can/bottle opener, wire stripper, lanyard attachment
Source: Leatherman, P. O. Box 20595, Portland, OR 97294, (503) 253-7826, www.leatherman.com

At the opposite end of the spectrum from the tiny Squirt is the Wave, Leatherman's most comprehensive multi-tool. Designed to be carried on the belt, in an equipment pouch, or on a utility pouch on a knife sheath, the Wave can be used for myriad tasks likely to arise in the field. Since it even includes a one-hand-opening knife blade it can replace the folding light utility knife as well. The two knife blades as well as the wood/metal file and the saw may be

SOG EOD Power Lock

SOG EOD PowerLock

leverage cap crimper for demolition usage. One aspect I find useful on the PowerLocks is the inclusion of scissors as well as pliers. Another feature which one appreciates more and more with use is the pivoting handle covers, which allow the pliers to be used much more comfortably. SOG offers variations in finish, including black oxide or gold TiNi. The latter titanium nitride finish is very scratch- and corrosion-resistant. For those who want a more compact tool, SOG also offers the Pocket PowerPlier.

Closed Length: 4.6 inches
Open Length: 7 inches
Weight: 9.5 ounces
Tools Included: Plier/gripper, wire cutters, crimper, wood saw, 1/2 serrated blade, 3-sided file, large screwdriver, Phillips screwdriver, _" driver, awl, can opener/small screwdriver, bottle opener/medium screwdriver, scissors, rulers and lanyard ring
Source: SOG, 6521 212th St, SW, Lynnwood, WA 98036, (425) 771-6230, www.sogknives.com

SOG offers a line of multi-tools that incorporate an interlocking gear system to produce compound leverage, which allows the PowerLock to perform surprisingly heavy tasks. This specific model also incorporates a compound

Cold Steel Bolo Machete

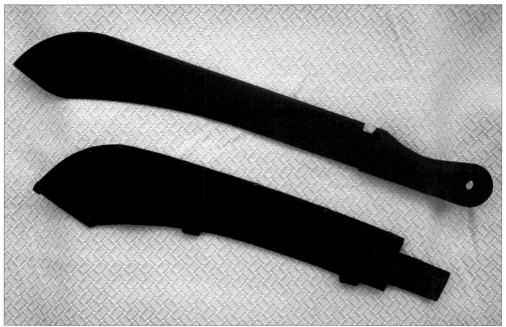

Cold Steel Bolo Machete

Overall Length: 22 inches
Blade Length: 16.4 inches
Weight: 17.3 ounces
Grip: Polypropylene, with large wrist-thong- or lanyard hole
Sheath: Black Cordura nylon, with slotted back, two retaining straps, steel safety toe
Source: Cold Steel, Inc., 3036-A Seaborg Ave., Ventura, CA 93003, (805) 650-8481, www.coldsteel.com

The Bolo machete is most often found throughout the Pacific Rim and Asia and has traditionally been a popular style in the USA dating from the long association of U.S. troops with the Philippines. The Bolo has a fat point which shifts the weight forward, helping this machete to perform heavy chopping very well. It is also extremely well balanced and has the reputation of being one of the most effective types of machetes if used for close combat.

Cold Steel Vietnam Tomahawk

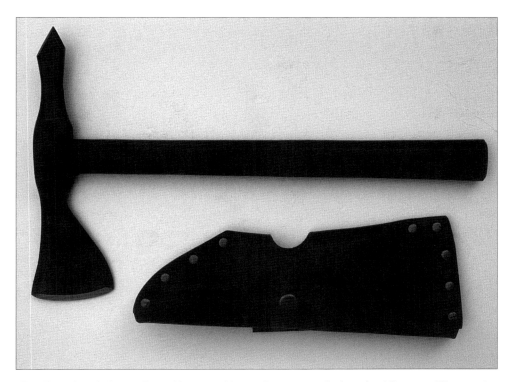

Afghanistan and Iraq. The primary edge is wide and upswept for cutting, slashing and chopping, while a secondary edge on the lower side of the head is curved and partially sharpened for cutting or hooking. A sharpened V-shaped spike at the back of the head may be used for devastating puncturing blows. Balanced to be head-heavy, the "Hawk" is very fast handling, though I do find the green wooden handle a bit slick and would recommend that friction tape or some other material be wrapped around it to form a grip.

Overall Length: 13.5 inches
Primary Edge: 3.5 inches
Weight: 19.1 ounces
Sheath: Leather
Source: Cold Steel, Inc., 3036-A Seaborg Ave., Ventura, CA 93003, (805) 650-8481, www.coldsteel.com

The Tomahawk has a long history with U.S. special operations troops, dating to the original Roger's Rangers. This traditional design was adapted for use by troops during the Vietnam War, and Cold Steel still makes this weapon available today, a weapon, it should be noted, which has seen use in both

Golok

Golok

The Golok has been a popular substitute for the machete in British Army service for many years, and is especially popular with members of the Special Air Service. Various contractors have, in fact, manufactured the Golok for the British Ministry of Defense. The design of the blade puts the weight forward to allow powerful chops. The Valiant Trading Company's version of the Golok as illustrated is a traditional example of this implement, which is widely used in Borneo and elsewhere in that region.

Overall Length: 20.5 inches
Blade Length: 14.5 inches
Weight: 19 ounces
Grip: Wood
Sheath: Decorated wood
Source: Valiant Trading Company, P.O. Box 648, Joundalup AC, WA 6919, Australia, Phone: +61-8-9304-0660, www.valiantco.com

Katz Safari Kit

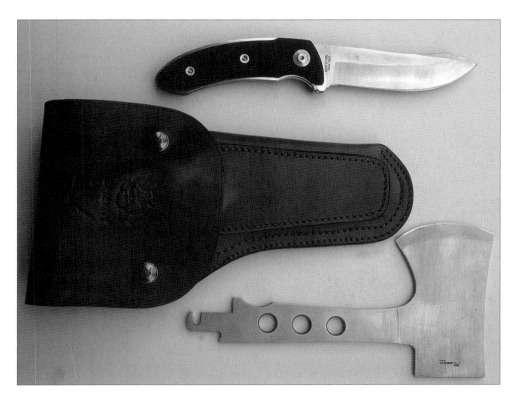

Katz Safari Kit

includes two saw blades, a boning-knife blade, and a filleting-knife blade, which may be installed in the handle. What makes the Safari Kit so appealing is that each piece is made with traditional Katz Knives quality. I am a fan of the Katz Kagemusha style, and find it highly desirable that a quality Kagemusha knife forms the basis for this kit.

Overall Length: Axe: 11.5 inches; knife: 9 inches
Knife Blade Length: 4 inches
Weight: 17.2 ounces
Grip: Kraton
Sheath: Leather for axe head and knife
Source: Katz Knives, P.O. Box 730, Chandler, AZ 85224, (480) 786-9334, www.katzkn@aol.com

The Safari Kit offers a very high quality axe/knife combination, which retains its very ergonomic grip by allowing the axe head or knife blade to be switched by releasing a retention lever. An accessory kit is also available which

Ontario Knife Company Cutlass Machete

Ontario Knife Company Cutlass Machete

most chores such as clearing undergrowth, etc., yet is still easily carried on the belt or pack and is quite well balanced in the hand.

Overall Length: 23.3 inches
Blade Length: 18 inches
Weight: 27 ounces
Grip: Polymer with handguard
Sheath: Ballistic nylon
Source: Ontario Knife Company, P.O. Box 145, Franklinville, NY 14737, (716) 676-5527, www.ontarioknife.com

This is a big heavy-duty machete with a 1095 carbon steel blade with a zinc phosphate finish and full tang construction. The D-shaped handguard protects the hand and makes the machete easier to handle. This machete is available in three blade lengths – 12 inches, 18 inches and 24 inches. The 18-inch example illustrated is my favorite as it is long enough to handle

Suggested Reading

Applegate, Rex. *Combat Use of the Double-Edged Fighting Knife.* (Boulder, CO: Paladin Press, 1993)

Bayonets. FM23-25, "War Department Basic Field Manual". (Washington: War Department, 1943)

Berner, Douglas C. *Survival Knife Reference Guide.* (Asheville, NC: Bee Tree Productions, 1986)

Brett, Homer M. *The Military Knife & Bayonet.* (Tokyo: World Photo Press, 2001)

Cole, M. H. *U.S. Military Knives, Bayonets and Machetes.* (Birmingham, AL: M.H. Cole, 1879)

Dick, Steven. *The Working Folding Knife.* (Wayne, NJ: Stoeger, 1998) Highly recommended and available from the author for $22.00 at Steven Dick, P.O. Box 538, Castle Rock, WA 98611

Flook, Ron. *British and Commonwealth Military Knives.* (Shrewsbury UK: Airlife, 1999)

Gaddis, Robert L. *Randall Made Knives: The History of the Man and the Blades.* (Boulder, CO: Paladin Press, 1993)

Ivie, Martin D. *Kalashnikov Bayonets: The Collector's Guide to Bayonets for the AK and Its Variations.* (Allen, TX: Diamond Eye Publications, 2002)

Janzen, Jerry L. *Bayonets from Janzen's Notebook.* (Broken Arrow, OK: Cedar Ridge Pubs, 1987)

Kane, Kathryn. *Swiss Army Knife Handbook: The Official History and Owner's Guide.* (Oracle, AZ: Birdworks Publications, 1988)

Langston, Richard V. *The Collector's Guide to Switchblade Knives.* (Boulder, CO: Paladin Press, 2001)

Marchington, James. *Knives: Military Edged Tools & Weapons.* ("Brassey's Modern Military Equipment", London: Brassey's, 1997)

McClung, Kevin. *ABC's of Steel Selection for Cutlery.* A web article at www.mdenterprise.com

McClung, Kevin. *Combat Knife Selection: Science in Action.* A web article at www.mdenterprise.com

McClung, Kevin. *Heat Treating the Blade.* A web article at www.mdenterprises.com

Peterson, Harold L. *Daggers and Fighting Knives of the Western World.* (New York: Bonanza Books, 1970)

Randall, W. D. Jr. and Rex Applegate. *Manual for the Use of Randall Made Fighting Knives and Similar Types.* (Orlando, FL: W. D. Randall Jr., no date)

Ripley, Tim. *Bayonet Battle: Bayonet Warfare in the Twentieth Century.* (London: Sidgwick & Jackson, 1999)

Sargeaunt, B.E. *Weapons: A Brief Discourse on Hand-Weapons Other than Firearms.* (London: Hugh Rees, Ltd., 1908)

Smith, J.E. Jr. *Combat-Fighting Knives.* (Statesboro, GA: EPJ&H Enterprises, 1987)

Smith, J.E. *Survival Knives and Survival.* (Statesboro, GA: EPJ&H Enterprises, 1984)

Stephens, Frederick J. *The Collector's Pictorial Book of Bayonets.* (Harrisburg: Stackpole, 1971)

Stone, George Cameron. *A Glossary of the Construction, Decoration, and Use of Arms and Armor.* (New York: Jack Brussel, 1961)

Thompson, Leroy. *Commando Dagger: The Complete Illustrated History of the Fairbairn-Sykes Fighting Knife.* (Boulder, CO: Paladin Press, 1985)

Thompson, Leroy. *Survival/Fighting Knives.* (Boulder, CO: Paladin Press, 1986)

Windrum, Dr. William. *Clandestine Edged Weapons.* (Williamstown, NJ: Phillips Publications, 2001)
Windrum, Dr. William. *The Earliest Commando Knives.* (Williamstown, NJ: Phillips Publications, 2000)

The Warrior's Edge. Six-volume video tape series. (Ventura, CA: Cold Steel, Inc., no date). Very comprehensive and available at www.coldsteel.com